Ever since I was a little girl and could barely talk, the word "why" has lived and grown along with me. It's a well-known fact that children ask questions about anything and everything, since almost everything is new to them. That was especially true of me, and not just as a child. Even when I was older, I couldn't stop asking questions.

I have to admit that it can be annoying sometimes, but I comfort myself with the thought that "You won't know until you ask," though by now I've asked so much that they ought to have made me a professor.

When I got older, I noticed that not all questions can be asked and that many whys can never be answered. As a result, I tried to work things out for myself by mulling over my own questions. And I came to the important discovery that questions which you either can't or shouldn't ask in public, or questions which you can't put into words, can easily be solved in your own head. So the word "why" not only taught me to ask, but also to think. And thinking has never hurt anyone. On the contrary, it does us all a world of good.

Anne Frank
in *Tales from the Secret Annex*

"She was born to be a writer. At thirteen, she felt the power; at fifteen, she was in command of it."

Cynthia Ozick in *The New Yorker*

". . . reminiscent of young Jane Eyre reading alone behind the curtains in the window-seat."

Jenny Diski in *Don't*

8/22

Bantam Books by Anne Frank

ANNE FRANK: THE DIARY OF A YOUNG GIRL

ANNE FRANK'S TALES FROM THE SECRET ANNEX

ANNE FRANK'S TALES FROM THE SECRET ANNEX

INCLUDING HER UNFINISHED NOVEL

Cady's Life

❦

EDITED BY GERROLD VAN DER STROOM
AND SUSAN MASSOTTY
TRANSLATED BY SUSAN MASSOTTY

(previously published in part as
Tales from the House Behind)

BANTAM BOOKS

ANNE FRANK'S TALES FROM THE SECRET ANNEX
A Bantam Book

PUBLISHING HISTORY

Portions of this book were previously published in The Works of Anne Frank *(Doubleday, 1959),* Tales from the House Behind *(Bantam, 1966), and* Tales from the Secret Annex *(Doubleday, 1983; Bantam, 1994).*

The complete and revised edition has now been published as Tales from the Secret Annex and Cady's Life *in* The Diary of Anne Frank: The Revised Critical Edition *(Doubleday, 2003).*

The revised paperback edition is available as Anne Frank's Tales from the Secret Annex *(Bantam, 2003).*

Published by Bantam Dell
A Division of Random House, Inc.
New York, New York

ISBN 0-553-58638-6
Manufactured in the United States of America
Published simultaneously in Canada

OPM   10   9   8   7   6   5   4

Contents

Explanatory Note

❀

Anne Frank is best known as the writer of her world-famous diary, though she tried her hand at other genres as well. Between September 1943 and May 1944, Anne wrote numerous stories, fairy tales, essays and personal reminiscences in a stiff-backed notebook reserved for that purpose. She did her utmost to make it resemble a real book, copying her stories neatly into the notebook and adding a title page, a table of contents, page numbers and so forth. Her collection of tales is now reproduced here in full, in a new translation, in the exact order in which she wrote them in her notebook.

Some of the sketches of life in the Secret Annex may already be familiar to readers of the diary, since Anne herself wrote several of these vignettes—sometimes with minor variations or on different dates—in her diary. These include: "Was There a Break-in?," "The Dentist," "Sausage Day," "Anne in Theory," "Evenings and Nights in the Annex," "Lunch Break" and "The Annex Eight at the Dinner Table," as well as one short story, "Kaatje."

Otto Frank, Anne's father, included even more of her

sketches in the first published edition of the diary: "The Best Little Table," "Wenn Die Uhr Halb Neune Schlägt . . . ," "A Daily Chore in Our Little Community: Peeling Potatoes!" and "Freedom in the Annex." In addition, the editor Mirjam Pressler included part of the sketch "Sundays" in the Definitive Edition of the diary.

Anne started to copy one story, "The Fairy," into her notebook, but never finished the task. Luckily, a complete version, written on loose sheets of paper, has survived. Since the fragment is nearly identical to the version on the loose sheets, only the latter is included here.

Similarly, four other stories, "Riek," "Jo," "Why?" and "Who Is Interesting?," were written only on loose sheets of paper. Because they are not dated, they are included here after "The Fairy," the last story in the notebook itself.

Anne also started a novel, which she called *Cady's Life*, at the back of Diary 2—the second volume of her diary— where there were still a number of blank pages. It is not known exactly when she began to write *Cady's Life*. However, from comments in her diary we can conclude that she must have been working on the "bits and pieces" during the first half of 1944. For one reason or another she never finished the novel, though in her diary entry of May 11, 1944, she briefly sketched the remainder of the plot.

Three fragments of *Cady's Life*, which were written on loose sheets of paper, have also been included in this edition. No attempt has been made to insert them in the proper chronological order in the story, since we have no way of knowing where—or indeed whether—Anne intended to include them. But because there is a gap in the chronology, the three fragments have been inserted before the final, very moving, piece in Anne's unfinished novel.

Interested readers are referred to *The Diary of Anne Frank: The Revised Critical Edition* (2003), which reproduces Anne Frank's *Tales from the Secret Annex* and *Cady's Life* in every detail. Gerrold van der Stroom's introduction to that section provides a wealth of background information.

Susan Massotty

Was There a Break-in?

Wednesday evening, March 24, 1943

Mother, Father, Margot and I were sitting quite pleasantly together when Peter suddenly came in and whispered in Father's ear. I caught the words "a barrel falling over in the warehouse" and "someone fiddling with the door."

Margot heard it too, but was trying to calm me down, since I'd turned white as chalk and was extremely nervous. The three of us waited. In the meantime Father and Peter went downstairs, and a minute or two later Mrs. van Daan came up from where she'd been listening to the radio. She told us that Pim* had asked her to switch it off and tiptoe upstairs. But you know what happens when you're trying to be quiet—the old stairs creaked twice as loud. Five minutes later Peter and Pim, the color drained from their faces, appeared again to relate their experiences.

They had positioned themselves under the staircase and waited. Nothing happened. Then all of a sudden they heard a couple of bangs, as if two doors had been slammed shut inside the house. Pim bounded up the

---

*Pim was Anne's nickname for her father.

stairs, while Peter went to warn Dussel, who finally presented himself upstairs, though not without kicking up a fuss and making a lot of noise. Then we all tiptoed in our stockinged feet to the van Daan family on the next floor. Mr. van D. had a bad cold and had already gone to bed, so we gathered around his bedside and discussed our suspicions in a whisper.

Every time Mr. van D. coughed loudly, Mrs. van D. and I nearly had a nervous fit. He kept coughing until someone came up with the bright idea of giving him codeine. His cough subsided immediately.

Once again we waited and waited, but heard nothing. Finally we came to the conclusion that the burglars had fled when they heard footsteps in an otherwise quiet building. The problem now was that the chairs in the private office were neatly grouped round the radio, which was tuned to England. If the burglars had forced the door and the air-raid wardens were to notice it and call the police, that would get the ball rolling, and there could be very serious repercussions. So Mr. van Daan got up, pulled on his coat and pants, put on his hat and cautiously followed Father down the stairs, with Peter (armed with a heavy hammer, to be on the safe side) right behind him. The ladies (including Margot and me) waited in suspense until the men returned five minutes later and told us that there was no sign of any activity in the building. We agreed not to run any water or flush the toilet, but since everyone's stomach was churning from all the tension, you can imagine the stench after we'd each had a turn in the bathroom.

Incidents like these are always accompanied by other disasters, and this was no exception. Number one: the

Westertoren bells stopped chiming, and they were always so comforting. Plus Mr. Voskuijl left early last night, and we weren't sure if he'd given Bep the key and she'd forgotten to lock the door.

Well, the night had just begun, and we still weren't sure what to expect. We were somewhat reassured by the fact that between eight-fifteen—when the burglar had first entered the building—and ten-thirty, we hadn't heard a sound. The more we thought about it, the less likely it seemed that a burglar would have forced a door so early in the evening, when there were still people out on the streets. Besides that, it occurred to us that the warehouse manager at the Keg Company next door might still have been at work. What with the excitement and the thin walls, it's easy to mistake the sounds. Besides, your imagination often plays tricks on you in moments of danger.

So we lay down on our beds, though not to sleep. Father and Mother and Mr. Dussel were awake most of the night, and I'm not exaggerating when I say that I hardly got a wink of sleep. This morning the men went downstairs to see if the outside door was still locked, but all was well!

Of course, we gave the entire office staff a blow-by-blow account of the incident, which had been far from pleasant. It's much easier to laugh at these kinds of things after they've happened, and Bep was the only one who took us seriously.

Note: The next morning the toilet was clogged, and Father had to stick in a long wooden pole and fish out several pounds of excrement and strawberry recipes (which is what we use for toilet paper these days). Afterward we burned the pole.

The Dentist

Wednesday, December 8, 1942

The nicest spectacle I've ever seen here took place today: Mother was ironing and Mrs. van Daan was scheduled for a dental appointment. Dussel began unpacking his case with an air of importance (it was the first time he'd worked on anyone here), and he needed some eau de cologne, which could be used as a disinfectant, and vaseline, which would have to do for wax. Mrs. van D. sat down, and he started looking in her mouth, but every time he touched a tooth, the poor woman flinched and uttered incoherent cries. After a lengthy examination (lengthy as far as Mrs. van D. was concerned, since it actually took no longer than two minutes), Dussel began to scrape out a cavity. But Mrs. van D. had no intention of letting him. She flailed her arms and legs until Dussel finally let go of his probe and . . . it remained stuck in Mrs. van D.'s tooth. That really did it! Mrs. van D. lashed out wildly in all directions, cried (as much as you can with an instrument like that in your mouth), tried to remove it, but only managed to push it in even farther. Mr. Dussel calmly observed the scene, his hands on his hips, while the rest of the audience roared with laughter. Of course, that was very mean of us. If it'd been me, I'm sure I would have yelled even louder. After a great deal of squirming, kicking, screaming and shouting, she finally managed to yank the thing out, and Mr. Dussel calmly went on with his work as if nothing had happened. He was so quick that Mrs. van D. didn't have time to pull any more shenanigans. But then, he had more help than he's ever had before: no fewer than two assistants; Mr. van D. and I performed our job well. The whole scene resembled one of those engravings from the Middle Ages, the kind showing a quack at work. In the meantime, however, the patient was getting restless, since she had to keep an eye on "her" soup and "her" food. One thing is certain: Mrs. van D. will never make another dental appointment!

Sausage Day

Friday, December 10, 1942

Mr. van Daan had a large amount of meat. Today he wanted to make bratwurst and sausages, and tomorrow mettwurst. It's fun watching him put the meat through the grinder: once, twice, three times. Then he adds all kinds of ingredients to the meat and uses a long pipe, which he attaches to the grinder, to force it into the casings. We ate the bratwurst with sauerkraut (served with onions and potatoes) for lunch, but the sausages were hung to dry over a pole suspended from the ceiling. Everyone who came into the room burst into laughter when they saw those dangling sausages. It was such a comical sight.

The place was a shambles. Mr. van Daan, clad in his wife's apron and looking fatter than ever, was concentrating his hefty form on the meat. What with his bloody hands, red face and apron, he really looked like a butcher. Mrs. van D. was trying to do everything at once: learn Dutch, cook, watch, sigh, moan—she claims to have broken a rib. That's what happens when you do such stupid physical exercises. Dussel had an eye infection and was sitting next to the stove dabbing his eye with chamomile tea. Pim, seated in the sunshine, kept having to move his chair this way and that to stay out of the way. His back must have been bothering him, because he was sitting slightly hunched over with an agonized expression on his face. He reminded me of those aged invalids you see in the poorhouse. Peter was romping around the room with the cat, holding out a piece of meat and then running off with the meat still in his hands. Mother, Margot and I were peeling potatoes. When you get right down to it, none of us were doing our work properly, because we were all so busy watching Mr. van Daan.

The Flea

❧

We're being plagued with yet another problem: Mouschi's fleas. We didn't know that people could be bitten by cat fleas, but they can.

Yesterday when I was upstairs I found a flea on my leg, ten minutes later when I was downstairs I nabbed another one, and last night when I was sitting on Dussel's bed, I felt another one crawling down my leg, but the little critter slipped through my fingers—they're incredibly fast. This morning I was getting dressed over by the closet when I saw another one of those wondrous creatures, walking along as pretty as you please. A flea that walks as well as jumps is a new experience for me. I picked it up and squeezed as hard as I could, but Mr. Flea hopped away again. Sighing, I got undressed and subjected my naked body and my clothes to a thorough examination until I finally found the flea in my panties. A second later, it was off with his head.

Do You Remember?

Memories of my schooldays at the Jewish Lyceum

Do you remember? I've spent many a delightful hour talking about school, teachers, adventures and boys. Back when our lives were still normal, everything was so wonderful. That one year of Lyceum was heaven to me: the teachers, the things I learned, the jokes, the prestige, the crushes, the admirers.

Do you remember? When I came back from town that afternoon and found a package in the mailbox from "*un ami, R.*" It could only have come from Rob Cohen. Inside there was a brooch worth at least two and a half guilders. Ultra-modern. Rob's father sold that kind of stuff. I wore it for two days, and then it broke.

Do you remember? How Lies and I told on the class. We had a French test. I wasn't having too much trouble with it, but Lies was. She copied my answers and I went over them to make corrections (on her test, I mean). She got a C+ and I got a C-, since thanks to my help she had gotten *some* things right, but both grades had been crossed out and replaced with a big fat F. Great indignation. We went to Mr. Premsela to explain what had happened, and at the end Lies said, "Yes, but the entire class had their books open under their desks!" Mr. Premsela promised the class that nobody would be punished if all those who had cheated would raise their hands. About ten hands went up—less than half the class, of course. A few days later Mr. Premsela sprang the test on us again. Nobody would talk to Lies and me, and we were branded as snitches. I soon caved in under the pressure and wrote a long letter of apology to Class 1 L II, begging their forgiveness. Two weeks later all had been forgotten.

The letter went something like this:

To the students in Class 1 L II,

Anne Frank and Lies Goslar hereby offer their sincere apologies to the students in Class 1 L II for their cowardly act of betrayal in the matter of the French test.

However, the deed was done before we had time to think, and we freely admit that we alone should have been punished. We believe that everyone is liable to let a word or sentence slip out in anger from time to time, and this can result in an unpleasant situation, even though it wasn't meant to. We hope that Class 1 L II will see the incident in this light and will repay evil with good. There's nothing more to be gained by it, and the two guilty parties can't undo what's been done.

We wouldn't be writing this letter if we weren't genuinely sorry for what happened. Furthermore, we ask those of you who have been ignoring us to please stop, since what we did wasn't so bad as to justify being looked upon as criminals for all eternity.

Anyone who is unable to put this matter behind them should come to us and either give us a good scolding or ask us for a favor, which we will gladly grant, if at all possible.

We trust that everyone in Class 1 L II will now be able to forget the affair.

Anne Frank and
Lies Goslar

Do you remember? How C.N.* told Rob Cohen in the streetcar, within earshot of Sanne Ledermann who passed it on to me, that Anne had a much prettier face than J.R., especially when she smiled. Rob's answer was, "Boy, have you ever got big nostrils, C.!"

Do you remember? How Maurice Coster was planning to present himself to Pim to ask his permission to see his daughter.

Do you remember? How Rob Cohen and Anne Frank exchanged a flurry of letters when Rob was in the hospital.

Do you remember? How Sam Solomon always followed me on his bicycle and wanted to walk arm in arm with me.

Do you remember? How A.W. kissed me on the cheek when I promised not to tell a soul about E.G. and him.

I hope that such happy, carefree schooldays will come again.

---

*Initials have been assigned at random to those persons wishing to remain anonymous.

The Best Little Table

Tuesday, July 13, 1943

Yesterday afternoon Father gave me permission to ask Dussel whether he would please be so good as to allow me (see how polite I am?) to use the table in our room two afternoons a week, from four to five-thirty. I already sit there every day from two-thirty to four while Dussel takes a nap, but the rest of the time the room and table are off-limits to me. It's impossible to study next door in the afternoon, because there's too much going on. Besides, Father sometimes likes to sit at the desk during the afternoon.

So it seemed like a reasonable request, and I asked Dussel very politely. What do you think the learned gentleman's reply was? "No." Just plain "No!"

I was incensed and wasn't about to let myself be put off like that. I asked him the reason for his "No," but this didn't get me anywhere. The gist of his reply was: "I have to study too, you know, and if I can't do that in the afternoons, I won't be able to fit it in at all. I have to finish the task I've set for myself; otherwise there's no point in starting. Besides, you aren't serious about your studies.

Mythology—what kind of work is that? Reading and knitting don't count either. I use that table and I'm not going to give it up!"

I replied, "Mr. Dussel, I do take my work seriously. I can't study next door in the afternoons, and I would appreciate it if you would reconsider my request!"

Having said these words, the insulted Anne turned around and pretended the learned doctor wasn't there. I was seething with rage and felt that Dussel had been incredibly rude (which he certainly had been) and that I'd been very polite.

That evening, when I managed to get hold of Pim, I told him what had happened and we discussed what my next step should be, because I had no intention of giving up and preferred to deal with the matter myself. Pim gave me a rough idea of how to approach Dussel, but cautioned me to wait until the next day, since I was in such a flap. I ignored this last piece of advice and waited for Dussel after the dishes had been done. Pim was sitting next door and that had a calming effect.

I began, "Mr. Dussel, you seem to believe further discussion of the matter is pointless, but I beg you to reconsider."

Dussel gave me his most charming smile and said, "I'm always prepared to discuss the matter, even though it's already been settled."

I went on talking, despite Dussel's repeated interruptions. "When you first came here," I said, "we agreed that the room was to be shared by the two of us. If we were to divide it fairly, you'd have the entire morning and I'd have the entire afternoon! I'm not asking for that much, but two afternoons a week does seem reasonable to me."

Dussel leapt out of his chair as if he'd sat on a pin. "You have no business talking about your rights to the room. Where am I supposed to go? Maybe I should ask Mr. van Daan to build me a cubbyhole in the attic. You're not the only one who can't find a quiet place to work. You're always looking for a fight. If your sister Margot, who has more right to work space than you do, had come to me with the same request, I'd never even have thought of refusing, but you . . ."

And once again he brought up the business about the mythology and the knitting, and once again Anne was insulted. However, I showed no sign of it and let Dussel finish: "But no, it's impossible to talk to you. You're shamefully self-centered. No one else matters, as long as you get your way. I've never seen such a child. But after all is said and done, I'll be obliged to let you have your way, since I don't want people saying later on that Anne Frank failed her exams because Mr. Dussel refused to relinquish his table!"

He went on . . . and on, until there was such a deluge of words I could hardly keep up. For one fleeting moment I thought, "Him and his lies. I'll smack his ugly mug so hard he'll go bouncing off the wall!" But the next moment I thought, "Calm down, he's not worth getting so upset about!"

At long last Mr. Dussel's fury was spent, and he left the room with an expression of triumph mixed with wrath, his coat pockets bulging with food.

I went running over to Father and recounted the entire story, or at least those parts he hadn't been able to follow himself. Pim decided to talk to Dussel that very same evening, and they spoke for more than half an hour. They first discussed whether Anne should be allowed to use the table, yes or no. Father said that he and Dussel had dealt with the subject once before, at which time he'd professed to agree with Dussel because he didn't want to contradict the elder in front of the younger, but that, even then, he hadn't thought it was fair. Dussel felt I had no right to talk as if he were an intruder laying claim to everything in sight. But Father protested strongly, since he himself had heard me say nothing of the kind. And so the conversation went back and forth, with Father defending my "selfishness" and my "busywork" and Dussel grumbling the whole time.

Dussel finally had to give in, and I was granted the opportunity to work without interruption two afternoons a week. Dussel looked very sullen, didn't speak to me for two days and made sure he occupied the table from five to five-thirty—all very childish, of course.

Anyone who's so petty and pedantic at the age of fifty-four was born that way and is never going to change.

Anne in Theory

Monday, August 2, 1943

Mrs. van Daan, Dussel and I were doing the dishes, and I was extremely quiet. This is very unusual for me, and they were sure to notice. So, in order to avoid any questions, I quickly racked my brains for a neutral topic. I thought the book *Henry from Across the Street* might fit the bill, but I couldn't have been more wrong. If Mrs. van D. doesn't jump down my throat, Mr. Dussel does. It all boiled down to this: Mr. Dussel had recommended the book to Margot and me as an example of excellent writing. We thought it was anything but that. The little boy had been portrayed well, but as for the rest . . . the less said the better. I mentioned something to that effect while we were doing the dishes, but my goodness . . . Dussel launched into a tirade.

"How can you possibly understand the inner life of a man? Of course you can follow that of a child [!]. But you're far too young to read a book like that. Even a twenty-year-old man would be unable to comprehend it." (So why did he go out of his way to recommend it to Margot and me?)

Mrs. van D. and Dussel continued their harangue: "You know way too much about things you're not supposed to. You've been brought up all wrong. Later on, when you're older, you won't be able to enjoy anything anymore. You'll say, 'Oh, I read that twenty years ago in some book.' You'd better hurry if you want to catch a husband or fall in love, since everything is bound to be a disappointment to you. [Get ready—here comes the best part.] You already know all there is to know in theory. But in practice? That's another story!"

Can you imagine how I felt? I astonished myself by calmly replying, "You may think I haven't been raised properly, but many people would disagree!"

They apparently believe that good child-rearing includes trying to pit me against my parents, since that's all they ever do. And not telling a girl my age about grown-up subjects is fine. We can all see what happens when people are raised that way.

At that moment I could have killed them both for poking fun at me. I was beside myself with rage, and counting the days until we no longer have to put up with each other's company.

Mrs. van D.'s a fine one to talk! She sets an example all right—a bad one. She's known to be exceedingly pushy, empty-headed and perpetually dissatisfied. Add to that, vanity and coquettishness and there's no question about it: she has a thoroughly despicable character. I could write an entire book about Madame van Daan, and who knows, maybe sometime I will. Deep down inside, she doesn't seem to have even one good trait. Anyone can put on a charming exterior when they want to. Mrs. van D. is friendly to men, so it's easy to make a mistake until you get to know her true nature. A good person can't imagine at first that she could be *so* cunning, *so* calculating and *so* selfish. It's impossible, you think, for anyone who looks reasonably well-bred on the outside to be so empty and bare on the inside.

Mother thinks that Mrs. van D. is too stupid for words, Margot that she's too unimportant, Pim that she's too ugly (literally and figuratively!), and after long observation (I'm not so distrustful at the beginning), I've come to the conclusion that she's all three of the above, and lots more besides. She has so many bad traits that I can't single out just one of them.

Will the reader please take into consideration that this story was written before the writer's fury had cooled?

The Battle of the Potatoes

Wednesday, August 4, 1943

After nearly three months of peace and quiet, interrupted by only a few quibbles, a fierce discussion broke out again today. It happened early in the morning, when we were peeling potatoes, and caught everyone off-guard. I'll give a rundown of the conversation, though it was impossible to follow it all since everyone was talking at once.

Mrs. van D. started it off (naturally!) by remarking that anyone who doesn't help peel potatoes in the morning should be required to do so in the evening. There was no reply, which apparently didn't suit the van Daans, since shortly after that Mr. van D. suggested that we all peel our own potatoes, with the exception of Peter, since peeling potatoes isn't a suitable chore for a boy. (Note the crystal-clear logic!)

Mr. van D. went on: "What I can't understand is why the men always have to help with the peeling. It means that the work isn't divided equally. Why should one person have to do more communal chores than another?"

Mother interrupted at this point, since she could see where the conversation was heading. "Aha, Mr. van Daan,

I know what comes next. You're going to tell us for the umpteenth time that the children aren't doing enough. But you know perfectly well that when Margot doesn't help out, Anne does, and vice versa. Peter never helps out as it is. You don't think it's necessary. Well, then, I don't think it's necessary for the girls to help either!"

Mr. van D. yelped, Mrs. van D. yipped, Dussel shushed and Mother shouted. It was a hellish scene, and there was poor little me watching as our supposedly "wise elders" literally fought it out.

The words flew thick and fast. Mrs. van D. accused Dussel of playing both sides against the middle (I quite agree), Mr. van D. spouted off at Mother, about the communal chores, about how much work he did and how we should actually feel sorry for him. Then he suddenly yelled, "It'd be better for the children if they helped out here a little more, instead of sitting around all day with their noses in a book. Girls don't need that much education anyway!" (Enlightened, huh?) Mother, having calmed down a little, declared that she didn't feel sorry for Mr. van Daan in the slightest.

Then he started in again. "Why don't the girls ever carry potatoes upstairs, why don't they ever haul hot water? They aren't that weak, are they?"

"You're crazy!" Mother suddenly exclaimed. I was actually pretty startled. I didn't think she'd dare.

The rest is relatively unimportant. It all boiled down to the same thing: Margot and I were supposed to be pressed into maid service in Villa Annex. In this case we might as well use the not-so-polite expression "stuff it," since it's never going to happen anyway.

Mr. van Daan also had the nerve to say that doing the

dishes, which Margot's done every morning and every evening for the last year, doesn't count.

When Father heard what had happened, he wanted to rush upstairs and give Mr. van D. a piece of his mind, but Mother thought it better to inform Mr. van D. that if everyone had to fend for themselves, they'd also have to live on their own money.

My conclusion is this: The whole business is typical of the van Daans. Always rubbing salt into old wounds. If Father weren't much too nice to people like them, it would be better to remind them in no uncertain terms that without us and the others they'd be facing death, in the truest sense of the word. In a labor camp you have to do a whole lot more than peel potatoes . . . or look for cat fleas!

Evenings and Nights in the Annex

❧

Wednesday, August 4, 1943

Just before nine in the evening: Bedtime always begins in the Annex with an *enormous* hustle and bustle. Chairs are shifted, beds pulled out, blankets unfolded—nothing stays where it is during the daytime. I sleep on a small divan, which is only five feet long, so we have to add a few chairs to make it longer. Comforter, sheets, pillow, blankets: everything has to be removed from Dussel's bed, where it's kept during the day.

In the next room there's a terrible creaking: that's Margot's folding bed being set up. More blankets and pillows, anything to make the wooden slats a bit more comfortable. Upstairs it sounds like bombs are falling, but it's only Mrs. van D.'s bed being shoved against the window so that Her Majesty, arrayed in her pink bed jacket, can sniff the night air through her delicate little nostrils.

Nine o'clock: After Peter's finished, it's my turn for the bathroom. I wash myself from head to toe, and more often than not I find a tiny flea floating in the sink (only during the hot months, weeks or days). I brush my teeth, curl my hair, manicure my nails and dab peroxide on my upper lip—all this in less than half an hour.

Nine-thirty: I throw on my bathrobe. With soap in one hand, and potty, hairpins, panties, curlers and a wad of cotton in the other, I hurry out of the bathroom. The next in line invariably calls me back to remove the gracefully curved but unsightly hairs that I've left in the sink.

Ten o'clock: Time to put up the blackout screen and say good-night. For the next fifteen minutes, at least, the house is filled with the creaking of beds and the sigh of broken springs, and then, provided our upstairs neighbors aren't having a marital spat in bed, all is quiet.

Eleven-thirty: The bathroom door creaks. A narrow strip of light falls into the room. Squeaking shoes, a large coat, even larger than the man inside it . . . Dussel is returning from his nightly work in Kugler's office. I hear him shuffling back and forth for ten whole minutes, the rustle of paper (from the food he's tucking away in his cupboard) and the bed being made up. Then the figure disappears again, and the only sound is the occasional suspicious noise from the bathroom.

Approximately three o'clock: I have to get up to use the tin can under my bed, which, to be on the safe side, has a rubber mat underneath in case of leaks. I always hold my breath while I go, since it clatters into the can like a brook down a mountainside. The potty is returned to its place, and the figure in the white nightgown (the one that causes Margot to exclaim every evening, "Oh, that indecent nighty!") climbs back into bed. A certain somebody lies awake for about fifteen minutes, listening to the sounds of the night: in the first place (when it's around three-thirty or four o'clock) to hear whether there are any burglars downstairs, and then to the various beds—upstairs, next door and in my room—to tell whether the others are asleep or half alert. This is no fun, especially when it concerns a roommate named Dr. Dussel. First, I hear the sound of a fish gasping for air, and this is repeated nine or ten times. Then, the lips are moistened profusely. This is alternated with little smacking sounds, followed by a long period of tossing and turning and rearranging the pillows. After five minutes of perfect quiet, the same sequence repeats itself three more times, after which he's presumably lulled himself back to sleep for a while.

Sometimes the guns go off during the night, between one and four. I'm never aware of it before it happens, but all of a sudden I find myself standing beside my bed, out of sheer habit. Occasionally I'm dreaming so deeply (of irregular French verbs or a quarrel upstairs) that I realize only when my dream is over that the shooting has stopped and that I've remained quietly in my bed. But usually I wake up. Then I grab a pillow and a handkerchief, throw on my robe and slippers and dash next door to Father, just the way Margot described in this birthday poem:

> *When shots ring out in the dark of night,*
> *The door creaks open and into sight*
> *Come a hanky, a pillow, a figure in white!*

Once I've reached the big bed, the worst is over, except when the shooting is extra loud.

Six forty-five: Brring . . . the alarm clock, which raises its shrill voice at any hour of the day or night, whether you want it to or not. Creak . . . wham . . . Mrs. van D. turns it off. Screak . . . Mr. van D. gets up, puts on the water and races to the bathroom.

Seven-fifteen: The door creaks again. Dussel can go to the bathroom. Alone at last, I remove the blackout screen . . . and a new day begins in the Annex.

Lunch Break

Thursday, August 5, 1943

It's twelve-thirty: The whole gang breathes a sigh of relief: Mr. van Maaren, the man with the shady past, and Mr. de Kok have gone home for lunch.

Upstairs you can hear the thud of the vacuum cleaner on Mrs. van D.'s beautiful and only rug. Margot tucks a few books under her arm and heads for the class for "slow learners," which is what Dussel seems to be. Pim goes and sits in a corner with his constant companion, Dickens, in hopes of finding a bit of peace and quiet. Mother hastens upstairs to help the busy little housewife, and I tidy up both the bathroom and myself at the same time.

Twelve forty-five: One by one they trickle in: first Mr. Gies and then either Mr. Kleiman or Mr. Kugler, followed by Bep and sometimes even Miep.

One: Clustered around the radio, they all listen raptly to the BBC. This is the only time the members of the Annex family don't interrupt each other, since even Mr. van Daan can't argue with the speaker.

One-fifteen: Food distribution. Everyone from downstairs gets a cup of soup, plus dessert, if there happens to be any. A contented Mr. Gies sits on the divan or leans against the desk with his newspaper, cup and usually the cat at his side. If one of the three is missing, he doesn't hesitate to let his protest be heard. Mr. Kleiman relates the latest news from town, and he's an excellent source. Mr. Kugler hurries up the stairs, gives a short but solid knock on the door and comes in either wringing his hands or rubbing them in glee, depending on whether he's quiet and in a bad mood or talkative and in a good mood.

One forty-five: Everyone rises from the table and goes about their business. Margot and Mother do the dishes, Mr. and Mrs. van D. head for the divan, Peter for the attic, Father for his divan, Dussel too, and Anne does her homework.

What comes next is the quietest hour of the day; when they're all asleep, there are no disturbances. To judge by his face, Dussel is dreaming of food. But I don't look at him long, because the time whizzes by and before you know it, it'll be four o'clock and the pedantic Dr. Dussel will be standing with the clock in his hand because I'm one minute late.

The Annex Eight at the Dinner Table

❧

Thursday, August 5, 1943

What is the scene around the table? How do the various table companions amuse themselves? One is noisy, the other quiet; one eats too much, the other too little, depending on their appetite.

Mr. van Daan: Is served first, and takes a generous portion of whatever he likes. Usually joins in the conversation, never fails to give his opinion. Once he's spoken, his word is final. If anyone dares to suggest otherwise, Mr. van D. can put up a good fight. Oh, he can hiss like a cat . . . but I'd rather he didn't. Once you've seen it, you never want to see it again. His opinion is the best, he knows the most about everything. Granted, the man has a good head on his shoulders, but it's swelled to no small degree.

Madame: Actually, the best thing would be to say nothing. Some days, especially when a foul mood is on the way, her face is hard to read. If you analyze the discussions, you realize she's not the subject, but the guilty party! A fact everyone prefers to ignore. Even so, you could call her the instigator. Stirring up trouble, now *that's* what Mrs. van Daan calls fun. Stirring up trouble between Mrs. Frank and Anne. Margot and Mr. Frank aren't quite as easy.

But let's return to the table. Mrs. van D. may think she doesn't always get enough, but that's not the case. The choicest potatoes, the tastiest morsel, the nicest bit of whatever there is, that's Madame's motto. The others can all have their turn, as long as I get the best. (Exactly what she accuses Anne Frank of doing.) Her second watchword is: keep talking. As long as somebody's listening, it doesn't seem to occur to her to wonder whether they're interested. She must think that whatever Mrs. van Daan does will interest everyone. Sometimes I think she's just like I used to be, though luckily I've changed and haven't stayed the same for forty-three years.

Smile coquettishly, pretend you know everything, offer everyone a piece of advice and mother them a bit—that's *sure* to make a good impression. But if you take a better look, the good impression fades. One, she's hardworking; two, cheerful; three, coquettish—and sometimes a cute face. That's Petronella van Daan.

The third diner: Says very little. Young Mr. van Daan is usually quiet and hardly makes his presence known. As far as his appetite is concerned, he's a Danaïdean vessel that never gets full. Even after the most substantial meal, he can look you calmly in the eye and claim he could have eaten twice as much.

Number four—Margot: Eats like a bird and doesn't talk at all. She eats only vegetables and fruit. "Spoiled," in the opinion of the van Daans. "Too little exercise and fresh air," in ours.

Beside her—Mama: Has a hearty appetite, but doesn't

live up to her potential. I always have the idea that people forget she's there, since she's off in the corner. Whenever the conversation turns to literature, you can learn a lot. She has a vast knowledge and is well read. No one has the impression, as they do with Mrs. van Daan, that she's a housewife. What's the difference between the two? Well, Mrs. van D. does the cooking and Mother does the dishes and polishes the furniture. Not that anyone takes much notice, but the rooms next door are clean as can be.

Numbers six and seven: I won't say much about Father and me. The former is the most modest person at the table. He always looks to see whether the others have been served first. He needs nothing; the best things are for the children. He's the model. Seated next to him is the canvas, which will hopefully turn out to be a good reproduction of the original.

Dussel: Help yourself, keep your eyes on the food, eat and don't talk. And if you have to say something, then for goodness' sake talk about good food. That doesn't lead to quarrels, just to bragging. He consumes enormous portions, and "no" is not part of his vocabulary, whether the food is good or bad.

Pants that come up to his chest, a red jacket, black patent-leather slippers and horn-rimmed glasses—that's how he looks when he's at work at the little table, always studying and never progressing. This is interrupted only by his afternoon nap, food and—his favorite spot—the bathroom. Three, four or five times a day there's bound to be someone waiting outside the bathroom door, hopping impatiently from one foot to another, trying to hold it in and barely managing. Does Dussel care? Not a whit. From seven-fifteen to seven-thirty, from twelve-thirty to one, from two to two-fifteen, from four to four-fifteen, from six to six-fifteen, from eleven-thirty to twelve. You can set your watch by them; these are the times for his "regular sessions." He never deviates or lets himself be swayed by the voices outside the door, begging him to open up before a disaster occurs.

Number nine: Is not part of our Annex family, although she does share our house and table. Bep has a healthy appetite. She cleans her plate and isn't choosy. Bep's easy to please and that pleases us. She can be characterized as follows: cheerful, good-humored, kind and willing.

Wenn Die Uhr Halb Neune Schlägt . . .*

❧

Friday, August 6, 1943

Margot and Mother are nervous. "Shh . . . Father. Be quiet, Otto. Shh . . . Pim! It's eight-thirty. Come here, you can't run the water anymore. Walk softly!" A sample of what's said to Father in the bathroom. At the stroke of half past eight, he has to be in the living room. No running water, no flushing toilet, no walking around, no noise whatsoever. As long as the office staff hasn't arrived, sounds travel more easily to the warehouse.

The door opens upstairs at eight-twenty, and this is followed by three gentle taps on the floor . . . Anne's hot cereal. I clamber up the stairs to get my doggie dish.

Back downstairs, everything has to be done quickly, quickly: I comb my hair, put away the potty, shove the bed back in place. Quiet! The clock is striking eight-thirty! Mrs. van D. changes shoes and shuffles through the room in her slippers; Mr. van D. too—a veritable Charlie Chaplin. All is quiet.

The ideal family scene has now reached its high point.

---

*"When the Clock Strikes Half-Past Eight" in German.

I want to read or study and Margot does too. Father and Mother ditto. Father is sitting (with Dickens and the dictionary, of course) on the edge of the sagging, squeaky bed, which doesn't even have a decent mattress. Two bolsters can be piled on top of each other. "I don't need these," he thinks. "I can manage without them!"

Once he starts reading, he doesn't look up. He laughs now and then and tries to get Mother to read a passage.

"I don't have the time right now!"

He looks disappointed, but then continues to read. A little while later, when he comes across another interesting bit, he tries again. "You *have* to read this, Mother!"

Mother sits on the folding bed, either reading, sewing, knitting or studying, whichever is next on her list. An idea suddenly occurs to her, and she quickly says, so as not to forget: "Anne, remember to . . . Margot, jot this down . . ."

After a while it's quiet again. Margot slams her book shut; Father knits his forehead, his eyebrows forming a funny curve and his wrinkle of concentration reappearing at the back of his head, and he buries himself in his book again; Mother starts chatting with Margot; and I get curious and listen too. Pim is drawn into the conversation . . .

Nine o'clock. Breakfast!

Villains!

❦

Friday, August 6, 1943

Who are the villains in this house? Real villains! The van Daans!

What is it this time?

Let me tell you.

The truth of the matter is that thanks to the indifference of the van Daans this house is crawling with fleas. For months we've been warning them, "Send your cat out to be sprayed!" Their answer was always, "Our cat doesn't have fleas!"

When the fleas had all too clearly been shown to exist and we all itched so much we couldn't sleep, Peter—who only felt sorry for the cat—went and had a look, and the fleas actually leapt up into his face. He went to work, combing the cat with Mrs. van D.'s fine-toothed comb, and brushing it with our one and only scrub brush. What was the result?

No fewer than a hundred fleas!

Mr. Kleiman was consulted, and the next day the downstairs rooms of the Annex were covered with a disgusting green powder. It didn't do a whit of good. So then we tried a spray gun with a kind of flea flit. Father, Dussel, Margot and I spent ages cleaning, mopping, scrubbing and spraying. The fleas had gotten into everything. We flitted everything in sight: clothes, blankets, floors, divans, every last nook and cranny.

Except upstairs and in Peter's room. The van Daans didn't think it was necessary. We insisted that they at least spray the clothing, bedding and chairs. They said they would. Everything was taken up to the attic and sprayed, or so they said. In reality, they did nothing of the kind! They apparently think it's easy to fool the Franks. Not one bit of spray; not one cloud of flit.

Their latest excuse: The flit would get into the food supplies!

Conclusion: It's their fault we have fleas. We're the ones that have to put up with the smell, the itch, the discomfort.

Mrs. van D. can't bear the stench at night. Mr. van D. pretends to flit, but brings the chairs, blankets, etc., back unflit. Let the Franks be bitten to death!

A Daily Chore in Our Little Community: Peeling Potatoes!

❧

Friday, August 6, 1943

One person goes to get some newspapers; another, the knives (keeping the best for himself, of course); the third, the potatoes; and the fourth, the water.

Mr. Dussel begins. He may not always peel them very well, but he does peel nonstop, glancing left and right to see if everyone is doing it the way he does. No, they're not.

"Look, Anne, I am taking peeler in my hand like so and going from top to bottom! *Nein*, not so . . . but so!"

"I think my way is easier, Mr. Dussel," I say tentatively.

"But this is best way, Anne. This you can take from me. Of course, it is no matter, you do the way you want."

We go on peeling. I glance at Dussel out of the corner of my eye. Lost in thought, he shakes his head (over me, no doubt), but says no more.

I keep on peeling. Then I look at Father, on the other side of me. To Father, peeling potatoes is not a chore, but precision work. When he reads, he has a deep wrinkle in the back of his head. But when he's preparing potatoes, beans or vegetables, he seems to be totally absorbed in his task. He puts on his potato-peeling face, and when it's set in that particular way, it would be impossible for him to turn out anything less than a perfectly peeled potato.

I keep on working. I glance up for a second, but that's all the time I need. Mrs. van D. is trying to attract Dussel's attention. She starts by looking in his direction, but Dussel pretends not to notice. She winks, but Dussel goes on peeling. She laughs, but Dussel still doesn't look up. Then Mother laughs too, but Dussel pays them no mind. Having failed to achieve her goal, Mrs. van D. is obliged to change tactics. There's a brief silence. Then she says, "Putti, why don't you put on an apron? Otherwise, I'll have to spend all day tomorrow trying to get the spots out of your suit."

"I'm not getting it dirty."

Another brief silence. "Putti, why don't you sit down?"

"I'm fine this way. I like standing up!"

Silence.

"Putti, look out, *du spritzt schon!*"*

"I know, Mommy, but I'm being careful."

Mrs. van D. casts about for another topic. "Tell me, Putti, why aren't the British carrying out any bombing raids today?"

"Because the weather's bad, Kerli!"

"But yesterday it was such nice weather and they weren't flying then either."

"Let's drop the subject."

"Why? Can't a person talk about that or offer an opinion?"

"No!"

_____

*"Now you're splashing!"

"Well, why in the world not?"

"Oh, be quiet, *Mammichen!*"*

"Mr. Frank always answers *his* wife." Mr. van D. is trying to control himself. This remark always rubs him the wrong way, but Mrs. van D.'s not one to quit.

"Oh, there's never going to be an invasion!" Mr. van D. turns white, and when she notices it, Mrs. van D. turns red, but she's not about to be deterred. "The British aren't doing a thing!" The bomb bursts.

"And now shut up, *Donnerwetter noch mal!*"† Mother can barely stifle a laugh, and I stare straight ahead.

Scenes like these are repeated almost daily, unless they've just had a terrible fight. In that case, neither Mr. nor Mrs. van D. says a word.

It's time for me to get some more potatoes. I go up to the attic, where Peter is busy picking fleas from the cat. He looks up, the cat notices it, and whoosh . . . he's gone. Out the window and into the rain gutter.

Peter swears; I laugh and slip out of the room.

---

*"Mommy!"

†"For crying out loud!"

Freedom in the Annex

Friday, August 6, 1943

Five-thirty: Bep's arrival signals the beginning of our nightly freedom. Things get going right away. I go upstairs with Bep, who usually has her dessert before the rest of us. The moment she sits down, Mrs. van D. begins stating her wishes. Her list usually starts with "Oh, by the way, Bep, something else I'd like . . ." Bep winks at me. Mrs. van D. doesn't miss a chance to make her wishes known to whoever comes upstairs. It must be one of the reasons none of them like to go up there.

Five forty-five: Bep leaves. I go down two floors to have a look around: first to the kitchen, then to the private office and then to the coal bin to open the cat door for Mouschi.

After a long tour of inspection, I wind up in Mr. Kugler's office.

Mr. van Daan is combing all the drawers and files for today's mail; Peter picks up Boche and the warehouse key; Pim lugs the typewriters upstairs; Margot looks around for a quiet place to do her office work; Mrs. van D. puts a kettle of water on the stove; Mother comes down the stairs with a pan of potatoes; we all know our jobs.

Soon Peter comes back from the warehouse. The first question they ask him is whether he's remembered the bread. No, he hasn't. He crouches before the door to the front office to make himself as small as possible and crawls on his hands and knees to the steel cabinet, takes out the bread and starts to leave. At any rate, that's what he intends to do, but before he knows what's happened, Mouschi has jumped over him and gone to sit under the desk.

Peter looks all around him. Aha, there's the cat! He crawls back into the office and grabs the cat by the tail. Mouschi hisses, Peter sighs. What has he accomplished? Mouschi's now sitting by the window licking herself, very pleased at having escaped Peter's clutches. Peter has no choice but to lure her with the bread. Mouschi takes the bait, follows him out, and the door closes.

I watch the entire scene through a crack in the door.

Mr. van Daan is angry and slams the door. Margot and I exchange looks and think the same thing: he must have worked himself into a rage again because of some blunder on Mr. Kugler's part, and he's forgotten all about the Keg Company next door.

Another step is heard in the hallway. Dussel comes in, goes toward the window with an air of propriety, sniffs . . . coughs, sneezes and clears his throat. He's out of luck—it was pepper. He continues on to the front office. The curtains are open, which means he can't get at his writing paper. He disappears with a scowl.

Margot and I exchange another glance. "One less page

for his sweetheart tomorrow," I hear her say. I nod in agreement.

We resume our work. An elephant's tread is heard on the stairway. It's Dussel, seeking comfort in his favorite spot.

We go on working. Knock, knock, knock . . . Three taps means dinnertime!

Kaatje

❧

Saturday, August 7, 1943

Kaatje is the girl next door. When I look out my window
during nice weather, I can see her playing in the garden.
Kaatje has a velvet burgundy-colored dress for Sundays
and a cotton one for weekdays. She has flaxen hair done
up in tiny little pigtails and bright-blue eyes.

Kaatje has a loving mother, but her father has passed
away. Kaatje's mother is a washerwoman. She's gone
sometimes during the day, cleaning other people's houses,
and when she comes home at night she does the laundry
for "her" people. At eleven o'clock she is still beating the
rugs and hanging row after row of washing on the line.

Kaatje has six brothers and sisters. One of them
screams and cries and latches on to his eleven-year-old
sister's skirts whenever their mother calls "Bedtime!"

Kaatje has a cat that's as black as a Moor; Kaatje takes
good care of her cat. Every evening, just before bedtime,
you can hear her calling, "Kat . . . je, kat . . . je."*

Which explains the name Kaatje. Maybe the little girl

---

*"Kitty, kitty."

next door isn't even called Kaatje, but she looks like she ought to be.

Kaatje also has two rabbits: a white one and a brown one. Hop . . . hop . . . hop, they jump and skip around in the grass at the foot of the steps to Kaatje's house.

Sometimes Kaatje is naughty, just like other children, especially when she and her brothers are having a quarrel. Oh, Kaatje can get angry all right. She can hit, kick and bite with the best of them. Her brothers have learned to respect their strong sister.

"Kaatje . . . ," Mother calls, "I need you to go to the store!" Kaatje quickly covers her ears so that she can honestly say she didn't hear her mother. Kaatje hates going to the store. But she wouldn't lie just to get out of it. Kaatje never lies. All you need to do is look into those blue eyes of hers to know she doesn't.

One of Kaatje's brothers is sixteen, and he works as an office boy. This brother sometimes bosses the younger children around as if he were their father. Kaatje doesn't dare talk back to Piet, because he's liable to smack her one and because she knows from experience that if you do what he says, he might give you a piece of candy. Kaatje likes candy, and so do her sisters.

On Sundays, when the church bells are going ding-dong-ding, Kaatje's mother and all her brothers and sisters go to church. Kaatje prays for her dear father, who's in Heaven, and also that her mother will live a long, long time. After church they all go out for a walk, which Kaatje enjoys a lot. They stroll through the park, and every once in a while they go to the zoo. But the zoo trip will have to wait for a few months, since they can only go again in September, when the admission price drops to twenty-five cents, or when Kaatje has a birthday. She's allowed to ask for an outing like that for her birthday, since it's the only kind of present her mother can afford.

Kaatje often has to comfort her mother, because, after a hard day of work, she sometimes falls exhausted into her chair at night and cries. So Kaatje promises to give her all the things she herself would like to have when she grows up. Kaatje wishes she were grown up already, so that she could earn money and buy beautiful clothes and give candy to her sisters, like Piet does. But first Kaatje has to go to school for years and years and learn all sorts of things.

Mother would like her to go to Housekeeping School, but Kaatje isn't keen on the idea. She doesn't want to work in a rich lady's house. She wants to work in a factory, like the girls who troop by her house every day. You aren't alone in a factory, you can chat with the others. And Kaatje loves to talk. At school she sometimes has to stand in the corner because she's been caught talking again, but otherwise she's a good student.

Kaatje adores her teacher, who's usually nice to her and is a very smart woman. You must have to work really hard to become that smart! But fewer brains will do. Kaatje's mother always says that if you're too smart, you won't find a husband, and Kaatje would hate that. After all, she wants to have children of her own one day, though not children like her brothers and sisters. Hers will be a lot nicer, and a lot better-looking. They'll have beautiful brown curly hair instead of her flaxen hair (which is horrible), and they won't have any freckles, which she has lots of. Nor does Kaatje want to have as many children as her mother did. Two or three will be enough. But, oh, she'll have to wait such a ve-ry long time—twice as long as she's lived so far.

"Kaatje," Mother calls. "Come here, you naughty little girl. Where have you been? Off to bed you go. I bet you've been daydreaming again!"

Kaatje sighs. Just when she'd been making such lovely plans for the future!

The Janitor's Family

❀

The janitor's family ignores the blackout regulations, both summer and winter. It looks like peacetime, when the lamps shone so invitingly in all the houses and you could see everyone gathered around the dining table or the tea table.

In this respect, the janitor's family doesn't seem to care whether it's war or peace. Take a look through the brightly lit window, and you'll see Father, Mother, Son and Daughter gathered around the table.

All Mother wants is to take as little notice of the war as possible. She doesn't like imitation gravy, so she does without, she doesn't want ersatz tea, so she drinks peppermint tea instead, and she doesn't want to hear the ack-ack guns, so she's come up with an effective remedy against that as well: she sits in the shower and listens to her loudest jazz record. And when the neighbors complain, she doesn't let it bother her, but brings them a peace offering in the form of food the next day.

The lady on the third floor, whose daughter is engaged to Son, gets a nice big pancake. And Mrs. Steen, the neighbor on her left, is favored with a quarter of a cup of sugar. The dentist in the second-floor apartment at the back, whose assistant is her youngest daughter, is not overlooked either. But Father is furious, since every ack-ack night costs him three cigarettes.

Mother and Father are alone during the daytime. They take loving care of their five rabbits, which get fatter every day. The rabbits have a cradle to sleep in, a shed to shelter from the rain in and a food bowl that serves as a dining table. In the wintertime they have a little house with windows and nice roomy cages. Their daily menu consists of carrot tops and other fine delicacies.

Father works hard in the garden, Mother in the house. Everything is spic and span. Once a week the windows are cleaned (both front and back), once a week the rugs are taken out and beaten and once a week the pots and pans are polished to a shine—all with the help of the fat cleaning lady who's worked for them forever.

Father's job has gotten easier. At the moment he takes care of just the big office upstairs. All he has to do is sleep lightly, so he can hear if anyone is trying to break in. In the old days Mother and the cleaning lady used to keep the entire building clean. However, she stopped working after one daughter got married and another had her tenth baby.

Mother and Father's biggest pleasure is having the grandchildren over for a visit. Their little voices ring out across the garden: "Grandma, Grandpa. Come look, the rabbits are doing such funny things!" And Grandma and

Grandpa rush over, because they believe that grandchildren ought to be spoiled. Grandchildren aren't like your own children, who need to be kept in line.

Grandpa is busy making a canoe for his oldest granddaughter's birthday. I wish I had a grandfather like him.

My First Day at the Lyceum

❀

Wednesday, August 11, 1943

After much wavering back and forth, discussion and debate, it was finally decided that I could attend the Jewish Lyceum and—after several more phone calls—that I could skip the entrance exams. I was a poor student in every subject, especially Math, and I was inwardly quaking at the thought of Geometry.

At the end of September, the long-awaited letter arrived, informing me that I was to enroll in the Jewish Lyceum on Stadstimmertuinen on such-and-such a date in October. When the appointed day came, it was pouring rain, which made it impossible for me to bike to school. So I took the streetcar, and of course I wasn't the only one.

As we approached the school, we could see a big crowd. Groups of girls and boys were standing around talking, and lots of them were strolling up and down and calling out, "Are you in my class?" "Hey, I know you!" "What class are you in?" Which is more or less what I did too. But except for Lies Goslar, I couldn't find a single friend who was going to be in my class. Hardly a comforting feeling.

School started, and we were welcomed to our classroom by a gray-haired teacher with a mousy face who was wearing a long dress and flat-heeled shoes. Surveying the busy scene and wringing her hands, she gave us the necessary information. Names were called, books were listed so they could be ordered, various other announcements were made and we were dismissed for the day.

To tell you the truth, it was disappointing. At the very least I had expected a class schedule and . . . the principal. I did see a short, fat, jolly man with ruddy cheeks in the hallway, nodding pleasantly to everyone as he talked to a thin man with glasses, thinning hair and a distinguished face, who wasn't much taller. But I had no idea that the former was the custodian and the latter the principal.

At home, I gave an excited account of the day's events. But when you get right down to it, I knew no more about the school, the students or the classes than I did before.

School was scheduled to start exactly one week after Enrollment Day. It was raining cats and dogs again, but I decided to ride my bike anyway. Mother stuck a pair of sweatpants in my schoolbag (heaven forbid I should get wet), and off we went.

Margot usually bicycles really fast. After two minutes, I was so out of breath that I had to ask her to please slow down. After another two minutes, there was such a downpour that, remembering Mother's warm sweatpants, I got off my bike and struggled my way into the garment—taking care not to let it drag through the puddle—then got back on my bike and set off with new determination. It didn't take long for me to start lagging behind again, so that once more I had to ask Margot to go slower.

She was a nervous wreck, and had already exclaimed the first time that she'd rather bike by herself from now on. No doubt scared of being late! But we got to school in plenty of time. After putting our bikes in the racks, we started chatting again as we walked through the passageway to the Amstel River.

The doors opened at eight-thirty on the dot. There was a big sign posted at the entrance, notifying everyone that about twenty students were being switched to another class. Of course I *would* have to be one of those twenty. According to the notice, I had been transferred to Class 1 L II. I knew a couple of the boys and some of the girls in this class, at least to speak to, but Lies was still back in Class 1 L I.

I felt quite forlorn, all by myself in my assigned seat in the last row, behind a bunch of tall girls. So, during the next period, I raised my hand and asked if I could move to another seat, since the only way I could see anything from behind those broad backs was to lean into the aisle. My request was immediately granted, so I picked up my meager belongings for the second time and moved to another seat.

Third period was gym. The teacher turned out to be so nice that I begged her to do what she could to get Lies transferred to my class. I don't know how she did it, but during the next period, in walked Lies. She was seated next to me.

After that, I was reconciled with the whole school. The school—which had given me so many advantages and so much pleasure—was now smiling down on me, and I began, my spirits soaring again, to pay attention to what the Geography teacher was saying.

A Biology Class

Wednesday, August 11, 1943

Wringing her hands, she comes into the room, wringing her hands, she sits down. She's forever wringing, wringing, wringing her hands.

Miss Biegel of Biology (gone are the days when it was called Natural History): a tiny woman with a big nose, blue gray eyes and gray hair, truly the face of a mouse or some other little creature.

In back of her, somebody carries in the chart and the skeleton. She goes over to stand behind the stove, wringing her hands again, and the class begins. First the homework review, then the lesson. Oh, she knows a lot, our Miss Biegel does. She tells a good story, about everything from fish to reindeer, but most of all (or so Margot says) she likes to talk and ask questions about reproduction. (Probably because she's an "old maid.")

All of a sudden her lecture is interrupted. A wad of paper flies through the room and lands on my desk.

"What have you got there?" Miss Biegel asked me in the unmistakable accent of someone from The Hague.

"I don't know, Miss Biegel!"

"Bring it here!"

Reluctantly, I got up from my desk and took the note up to the front.

"Who threw it?"

"I don't know, Miss Biegel. I haven't read it yet."

"Oh. Then we'll start by finding out what it says."

She unfolded the note and let me read what was written on it. There was only one word: "snitch." I turned red. She looked at me.

"So now do you know who threw it?"

"No, Miss Biegel."

"That's a lie!"

I turned bright red and glared at her, my eyes flashing, but I didn't say a word.

"I want to know who wrote it. Whoever it was, raise your hand!"

A hand went up in the back of the room. Just as I suspected—Rob Cohen.

"Rob, come here!" Rob came.

"Why did you write that?"

Silence.

"Do you know what it refers to, Anne?"

"Yes, Miss Biegel."

"Tell me!"

"Can't we discuss it another time, Miss Biegel? It's a long story."

"No, I want to hear it now!"

So I told her about the F I'd gotten for cheating on the French test and about telling on the rest of the class.

"That's a delightful tale! Rob, couldn't you wait until after class to give Anne the benefit of your opinion? As for you, Anne, I find it difficult to believe that you didn't know who threw the note. Go back to your seats!"

I was furious. When I got home I recounted the entire incident, and later, when an opportunity to get back at Miss Biegel presented itself, I sent Father to deal with her.

He came home with the news that he had called her Miss Biggel the whole time. According to her, Anne Frank was a very nice girl, and she had no recollection of having said I'd lied!

A Math Class

❦

Standing before the class, he's an impressive figure: tall, old, always in the same gray suit with a wing collar, a bald head with a wreath of gray hair. Speaks a strange dialect, grumbles a lot, laughs a lot. Patient when you try, short-tempered when you're lazy.

Nine out of the ten children he calls on don't know the answer. Over and over again, he explains, describes and demonstrates how to arrive at a number below zero. He loves asking riddles, is fun to talk to after class and used to be chairman of a large soccer club.

Mr. Keesing and I were often at loggerheads when it came to . . . talking in class. In the space of three days, I got six warnings. He was so fed up that he assigned me the usual two-page essay. I turned it in during the next Math class, and Mr. Keesing, who can take a joke, laughed heartily at my essay, which had a paragraph in it that went something like this: "I should indeed try hard to break myself of the habit of talking, but I'm afraid there isn't much I can do about it, since it's a hereditary disease. Because my mother also loves to talk, I assume I must have gotten it from her. So far, she hasn't been cured of the habit either." The topic of the assigned essay was "A Chatterbox."

During the next class, however, another opportunity for a cozy chat presented itself . . . Mr. Keesing went over to his book and wrote, "Miss Anne Frank: an essay entitled 'An Incorrigible Chatterbox.' Due tomorrow."

As behooves a good student, I duly handed in this essay too, but the malady struck again during the next class, whereupon Mr. Keesing wrote in his book, "Miss Anne Frank: a two-page essay entitled '"Quack, Quack, Quack," Said Mistress Chatterback.'"

What could I come up with now? I realized all too well that it was meant in fun, as otherwise he would have assigned me extra math problems, so for that reason I took the bull by the horns and answered his joke with a joke of my own, i.e., by writing my essay (with Sanne Ledermann's help) in verse. The first part went like this:

> "Quack, quack, quack," said Mistress Chatterback,
> Calling her ducklings from the deep.
> And up they came, "Cheep, cheep, cheep
> Well, do you have any bread for us,
> For Gerald, Mina and Little Gus?"
> "Why, yes, of course I do,
> A lovely crust I stole for you.
> It's all I could find, you'll have to share,
> Now please divide it fair and square!"
> So, following their mom's advice,
> They did their best to be precise,
> Eating and calling, "Cluck, cluck, cluck,
> My piece is bigger, I'm in luck!"

But, oh, along came Papa swan,
Scowling at their noisy goings-on.
Etc., etc.

Keesing read it, then read it out loud to the class, and again to a couple of other classes, and finally called it quits. From that moment on, I was given a lot of leeway. He overlooked my chatter and never punished me again.

P.S. This shows what a good-humored man he was. Thanks to Mr. Keesing, everybody calls me Mistress Chatterback.

Eva's Dream

Wednesday, October 6, 1943

Part 1

"G'night, Eva. Sleep tight."

"You too, Mom."

Click went the light, and Eva lay for a few moments in the darkness. Once her eyes had gotten used to it, she noticed that her mother hadn't closed the curtains all the way—there was a strip of light in the middle, through which she could see the plump round face of the moon. The moon hung motionless in the sky, calm and with a constant smile on his face, friendly to one and all.

"If only I could be like that," Eva whispered to herself. "I wish I were calm and friendly all the time, so that everybody would think I was a nice little girl. Oh, wouldn't that be lovely!"

Eva thought and thought about the moon, and about the glaring difference between the moon and herself. Finally, after all that thinking, her eyelids closed and her thoughts transformed themselves into a dream, which

Eva remembered in such detail the next day that she later wondered if it had actually happened.

Eva found herself at the entrance to a large park. She was peering uncertainly through the gate, not quite daring to go inside. Just as she was about to turn away, a tiny little woman with wings came up to her and said, "Don't be afraid to go in, Eva. Or don't you know the way?"

"No, I don't," Eva shyly confessed.

"Well, then, let me show you." And the plucky little elf took Eva's hand.

Eva had gone for many walks in many different parks with her mother and grandmother, but she had never seen one as beautiful as this. There were masses of flowers, trees and fields, every imaginable kind of insect, and small animals such as turtles and squirrels.

The elf chatted about cheerful things until Eva finally overcame her bashfulness enough to ask a question. But the elf quickly silenced her by putting a finger to Eva's lips.

"I'll point out everything in turn and explain it to you. After each explanation you can ask me questions about the things you don't understand, but the rest of the time you'll have to keep quiet and not interrupt. If you do, I'll take you home at once, and then you'll be just as ignorant as all the other ignorant people!

"Well, that's that. Let's begin. First, there's the rose— the queen of the flowers; she's so beautiful and her fragrance is so intoxicating that it goes to everyone's head, most of all her own. The rose is beautiful, sweet-smelling and elegant, but if things aren't going her way, she shows her thorns. She's like a spoiled child—beautiful, elegant and seemingly nice as can be, but if you touch her or talk to someone else so that she's no longer the center of attention, out come her claws. She'll be catty and offended, and will do her best to hide it. Her manners have been acquired, which means they're only skin-deep."

"But, Elf, if that's true, why does everyone think of the rose as the queen of the flowers?"

"Most people are blinded by the outer glow. If they'd been allowed to vote, very few people would have picked the rose. The rose is majestic and beautiful, and just as in the real world, no one asks the flowers whether a bloom which is outwardly less pretty might actually be inwardly more beautiful and more fit to rule."

"Do you mean to say, Elf, that the rose isn't beautiful?"

"Not at all, Eva. The rose *is* beautiful on the outside. And if she weren't constantly in the limelight, she might even be nice and kind. But since she happens to be first and foremost among the flowers, she will always think she's prettier than she actually is, and as long as that's true, the rose will go on being stuck-up, and I don't like stuck-up creatures!"

"Is Leentje stuck-up? After all, she's beautiful and rich, which is why she's our class's ringleader."

"Think about it for a moment, Eva. You'll have to admit that if your classmate Marietje were to stand up to her, Leentje would soon have all the other girls on her side. She'd point out that Marietje is ugly and poor. The rest of you would do whatever Leentje tells you to, because you all know she'll be mad at you if you don't, and that you'll never be able to get in her good graces again. And in your eyes, being out of your ringleader's good graces is almost as bad as having the principal mad at you. You wouldn't be allowed to go to her house anymore, and the rest of the class would ignore you. Later on, girls like Leentje will find themselves alone, because when the other girls are older, they'll turn against her. But, Eva, if they were to do that now, Leentje would have an opportunity to change before she winds up being alone for the rest of her life."

"Should I try to get the other girls to stop listening to her?"

"Yes. She'll be angry and indignant at first. But once she realizes why you're doing it and understands her own behavior better, she'll be grateful and will have more genuine friends than she's ever had before."

"Now I see what you mean. But tell me, Elf, am I also vain, like the rose?"

"Listen to me, Eva. Any adult or child who seriously asks themselves that question can't be vain, because vain people don't realize they're vain. You're the best person to answer that question, so I advise you to look into your own heart.

"But let's continue. You see this? Isn't it nice?" As she spoke, the elf knelt beside a bluebell, which was gently swaying back and forth in the grass to the rhythm of the wind.

"This bluebell is simple and kind. It brings joy to the world. It chimes for flowers, just as church bells chime for people. It helps lots of flowers and is a comfort to them. The bluebell is never lonely; there's music in its heart. It's a much happier creature than the rose. The bluebell isn't interested in the praise of others. The rose lives and thrives on admiration. When that's missing, the rose has nothing to make her happy. Her outward appearance is for other people, but her heart is empty and therefore cheerless. The bluebell, on the other hand, may not be as beautiful, but she has 'real' friends who value her melodies; those friends live in the flower's heart."

"But the bluebell is also a pretty flower, isn't it?"

"Yes, but not as eye-catching as the rose. Unfortunately, most people only notice the most obvious things."

"But I often feel lonely too and want to have people around me. Is that wrong?"

"That has nothing to do with it, Eva. Later, when you're older, you'll hear the song in your heart. I'm sure you will!"

"Please continue your story, dear little elf. It's beautiful, and so are you."

"Okay, I'll go on. Next, I want you to look up!" With her tiny index finger, the elf pointed up at a large, stately, old chestnut tree. "It's an impressive tree, isn't it?"

"Yes, and so big. How old do you think it is, Elf?"

"At least a hundred and fifty years old. But he's still standing tall, and he doesn't feel old. Everyone admires him for his strength, and he proves it by taking no notice of their admiration. He won't tolerate having anyone higher, and he's egotistical and indifferent to others—as long as *he* has what he wants, nothing else matters. He looks so generous, our chestnut does, as if he's a comfort to one and all, but it's easy to be mistaken. The chestnut would rather not have anyone come to him with their troubles. He leads a good life, but begrudges others the same. The trees and flowers know it, so they take their troubles to the cozy, comfy pine tree and ignore the chestnut.

"Still, the chestnut tree has a very small song in a very big heart. This can be seen by his affection for the birds.

There's always a place for them on one of his branches, and he always has a little something for them, even if it's not much."

"Is it all right if I compare the chestnut tree to a certain type of person?"

"There's no need for you to ask, Eva. All living creatures can be compared to one another. The chestnut tree is no exception. Anyway, he's not all bad, he's just not particularly good to people. But he harms no one. He leads his own life, and is happy. Do you have any other questions, Eva?"

"No, I understand everything you said and I'm very grateful for your explanations, Elf. I have to go home now, but will you please come again someday and tell me more?"

"I'm afraid that's impossible. Sleep tight, Eva."

And the elf was gone. Eva woke up, just as the moon was making way for the sun and the neighbor's cuckoo clock was cheeping seven.

Part 2

The dream made a deep impression on Eva. Nearly every day she noticed some disagreeable things about herself, then remembered the elf's advice.

She also tried hard not to let Leentje have her way all the time. But girls like Leentje know at once when someone has it in for them or tries to topple them from their throne. So, whenever Eva suggested that another person take the lead in one of their games, Leentje defended herself with all her might. Her "faithful followers" (the girls who had decided to stick with Leentje through thick and thin, or so they promised) were encouraged to rebel against "that bossy Eva." But Eva noticed to her delight that this time Leentje was less sure of herself than she had been with Marietje.

Marietje was small, thin and timid. Eva was amazed that she even dared stand up to Leentje. As she got to know her better, Eva saw that Marietje would actually be a lot nicer and a lot more fun to have as a friend than Leentje.

Eva didn't breathe a word of the elf's visit to her mother. She wasn't sure why, since up to now she'd shared everything with her mother, but for the first time she felt the need to keep it to herself. She couldn't explain it, but she had the feeling that her mom wouldn't understand. The elf was so beautiful and Mom hadn't been there in the park or seen the elf. Eva wouldn't be able to describe what the elf looked like.

It didn't take long for the dream to have such an effect on Eva that her mother noticed how different she was. Eva talked about other, more important things, and didn't get so upset about trivial things. But she hadn't told her mother the reason for her remarkable change, and her mother didn't dare push her to confide.

So Eva lived her life, thinking of the elf's good advice and accumulating more all the time. She never again saw another trace of the elf. Leentje was no longer the ring-leader. Each of the girls took turns. At first Leentje had been very angry, but when she noticed that it didn't help, she adopted a friendlier attitude. In the end everyone wound up treating her normally, because she didn't fall back into her bad habits again.

At that point, Eva decided to tell her mother the whole story. Somewhat to her surprise, her mom didn't laugh, but said, "The elf accorded you a great privilege, my dear. I doubt whether she thinks very many girls and boys are ready to listen to her. Be equally cautious with your trust, and tell no one else what happened. You must always do what the elf told you to do, and never, ever forget her advice."

As Eva grew older, she did a lot of good things for those around her. At the age of sixteen (four years after meeting the elf), she was generally acknowledged to be a friendly, gentle and helpful girl. Every time she did something good, she felt happy and warm inside, and she gradually came to understand what the elf had meant by "the song in her heart."

One day when she was an adult, the image of the elf flashed through her mind and she suddenly realized who and what the elf had been. All at once she felt sure it had been her own conscience, showing her in her dream what was right. But she was deeply grateful that she'd had the elf as her example in her childhood.

Roomers or Renters

Friday, October 15, 1943

When the time came to decide whether or not to rent out our big back room, we had to fight hard to overcome our pride, for who is used to having a stranger, much less a paying one, in the house?

But when times are hard and the rent is badly needed, you have to put aside your pride, and lots more besides. Which is just what we did. The back bedroom was cleared out and furnished with odds and ends, though there were far too few of those for the stylish bed-sitting-room we had in mind.

So my father set forth, poking around auctions and public sales, coming home one day with this gem, and the next day with that one. After three weeks, we had a pretty wastepaper basket and an adorable tea table, but we still needed two armchairs and a decent wardrobe.

My father set out again. This time, as a special treat, he took me along. We arrived at the auction hall and sat down on a row of wooden benches, next to a couple of frazzled junk dealers and assorted shady characters. We waited, and waited, and waited. We could have waited till a new day dawned, because they were auctioning only porcelain that day!

Disappointed, we retraced our steps, only to return the next day, not very hopeful, to try again. But . . . this time we were in luck, and my father was able to snap up a really beautiful oak wardrobe and two leather club chairs. To celebrate our new purchases and what we hoped would be the speedy arrival of our roomer, we treated ourselves to tea and cake and went home in good spirits.

But, oh woe, when the armchairs and wardrobe arrived the next day and had been moved into the room, my mother discovered that the wardrobe had these strange little traces of sawdust. My father took a look . . . and found that it was indeed riddled with woodworm. It's just the kind of thing they don't put on the tag, nor is it possible to see these things in a dark auction hall.

After this discovery, we took a better look at the armchairs. Surprise, surprise, they were also infested with woodworm. We called the auction hall and asked them to pick up the items as soon as possible. They came, and my mother heaved a sigh of relief when the auction furniture was finally out the door. My father couldn't help sighing either—at the thought of how much money he had lost.

A few days later, my father ran into a friend who had a few pieces of furniture he was willing to lend us until we could find something better. So the problem was finally solved.

Then we sat down and wrote an ad to be hung in the window of the bookstore on the corner, and agreed to pay for it to be posted for a week. Soon people were coming to look at the room. The first one was an elderly gentleman hoping to find a place for his unmarried son. Everything was almost settled when the son himself spoke up, and he said such crazy things that my mother seriously began to wonder if he had all his marbles. She was right, since the elderly gentleman hesitantly admitted that his son was a bit out of the ordinary. You wouldn't believe how fast she showed those two the door.

Dozens of people came and went, until one day the door opened to a short, fat, middle-aged man who was willing to pay a lot and had few demands, so he was quickly accepted. This gentleman actually gave us more pleasure than trouble. Every Sunday he brought chocolate for the children and cigarettes for the adults, and more than once he took us all to the movies. He stayed with us for one and a half years, then moved into his own apartment, together with his mother and sister. Later, he used to drop by from time to time and swear that he'd never had such a good time as he'd had with us.

Once more we put an ad in the window and once more our doorbell was rung by young and old, short and tall. One of them was a fairly young woman wearing the same kind of bonnet they wear in the Salvation Army, so we quickly dubbed her "Salvation Army Josephine." She got the room, but she wasn't as nice to share the house with as the fat man. First of all, she was terribly messy, leaving things all over the place. Second, and more important, she had a fiancé who was often drunk, and he was even less charming to have around. One night, for instance, we were startled out of our sleep by the doorbell. My father got up to take a look and found himself confronted with the inebriated fiancé, who kept clapping him on the shoulder and saying, over and over again, "We sure are pals, aren't we? Yep, we sure are pals!" Wham . . . the door was slammed in his face.

When the war broke out in May 1940, we gave her notice and rented the room to a thirty-year-old man of our acquaintance who was also engaged. He was nice, but he had one failing: he was terribly spoiled. One time, during the winter, when we were having to economize on the electricity, he complained bitterly of the cold—a shameful exaggeration, since the heat in his room was turned up as high as it would go. But you have to humor your roomers sometimes, so he was given permission to switch on the electric heater occasionally for an hour or two. What do you think he did? He kept that heater turned to "Hot" all day long. We begged and pleaded with him to economize a bit, but it didn't help. The electricity meter kept ticking faster and faster, so one day my fearless mother took the fuse out of the box and disappeared for the rest of the afternoon. She then blamed the heater for supposedly blowing the fuse, and the young man was obliged to sit in the cold. Nevertheless, he was also with us for one and a half years, until he left to get married.

Once again the room was empty. My mother was about to place another ad when a friend called up and foisted a divorced man on us who was in urgent need of a room. He was a tall man, about thirty-five years old, with glasses and a very unpleasant face. We didn't want to disappoint our friend, so we rented the room to him. He too was engaged, and his fiancée often came to the house.

Not long before the wedding they quarreled and broke up, and he rushed headlong into a marriage with someone else.

Right about then we moved and finally got rid of our roomers (hopefully once and for all)!

Paula's Flight

Wednesday, December 22, 1943

In the old days, when I was a little girl, Pim used to tell me stories about "Der bösen Paula."* He had a whole collection of Paula stories, and I adored them all. Now, whenever I go to him for comfort in the middle of the night, he's started telling me Paula stories again, so I've written down the latest one.

Chapter 1

For a long time, Paula had been trying to work out a way to see the inside of an airplane. Her father had recently gotten a job at an airport near Berlin, and Paula and her mother had moved there to be with him.

One fine day, when things were fairly quiet at the airport, she summoned every ounce of courage she had and climbed into the first plane she happened to see. She inspected every nook and cranny, taking her own sweet time, before finally pausing in fascination outside the cockpit. She was just about to reach for the doorknob

---

*"The Bad Paula."

when, to her indescribable horror, she heard voices outside. She quickly crawled under one of the benches and waited tremblingly to see what was going to happen next.

The voices came closer and closer, and a moment later she saw two men step into the plane. They walked back and forth, nearly bumping into the bench under which she was crouched. Then the two men sat down on one of the benches behind her and started speaking in such a strange dialect that Paula couldn't understand a word. After about fifteen minutes, they stood up and one of them left the plane. The other one shut himself in the cockpit, only to come out again dressed as a pilot. Then the second man came back, followed by six other men, and they all climbed aboard. Paula, still shaking, listened as the engine was switched on and the propellers began to turn.

Chapter 2

Despite her daring, Paula was often cowardly and afraid, though sometimes she could be unexpectedly brave, so that no one was able to predict which of these two opposites was going to come to the fore. This time she was extraordinarily brave, because, after they had flown for a while, she suddenly crawled out from under the bench and, to the infinite astonishment of the crew, introduced herself and told them how she got there. The crew discussed what they should do with Paula and decided that they had no choice but to keep her with them. They told her that they were on their way to Russia to bomb the enemy lines.

Sighing, she lay down on a bench and went to sleep. Bang-bang, boom-boom . . . Paula sat up immediately

and stared wide-eyed at the crew. No one had time to
deal with her, though, because the Russians were shooting fast and furiously at the enemy aircraft. Suddenly . . .
Paula screamed, the benches shook and the windows rat-
tled as a couple of shells slammed into the plane and sent
it into a nosedive, so that they were forced to make an
emergency landing.

As soon as the plane hit the ground, some Russians
raced over and put handcuffs on the entire crew. You can
imagine the looks on their faces when they suddenly saw
a little thirteen-year-old girl standing before them. Neither the Russians nor the Germans understood a word of
each other's language, so a young Russian took Paula's
hand and walked with her behind the crew all the way
to the prison camp. The camp's commander burst into
laughter when he saw Paula standing calmly before him.
But since he didn't want to take the little girl prisoner, he
decided to make inquiries behind the lines the following
day until he found a simple family who would care for her
until after the war.

Chapter 3

One rainy day, after she had spent about a week in the
commander's office, Paula was bundled, just as she was,
into a big car that was taking wounded soldiers to the
hospital. The car bumped and bounced over the cobblestones for a full five hours, while outside a curtain of rain
blocked her view. An occasional cottage dotted the deso-
late landscape, but they all seemed to be deserted. At the
beginning of their trip, they could still hear the steady

roar of the distant cannons, but the sound gradually got weaker and weaker until it finally died away completely.

Suddenly there was more traffic on the road. They passed several cars, then stopped in front of a white house with red crosses painted all over it. The wounded were taken out of the car and carried inside, where friendly nurses were waiting to receive them.

After all of the men had been unloaded, the driver drove on without a word. A whole hour went by before he stopped again. Through the trees Paula saw a fairly large farmhouse. The driver gestured in the direction of the house, and Paula understood that she was supposed to get out.

She stood on the road, waiting for the driver, but before she knew what had happened, the car had driven off, leaving her alone on the empty road. "What strange people the Russians are," Paula thought. "Here I am, left to my fate in a foreign country. If the tables were turned, no German would act this way!" (Don't forget that Paula was German.) She suddenly remembered, however, that the driver had pointed to the house. So she crossed the road, opened the gate and found herself in a sort of fenced-in pasture. In front of the house she spied a woman doing the laundry and a little girl hanging sheets on the line.

Holding out her hand, she walked over to the woman and murmured, "Paula Müller." The woman looked up, shook Paula's hand, after first wiping her own on her soaking-wet apron, and said, "*Ustichyaraya kolovnya.*" Paula assumed that this was the woman's name, though it simply meant "Welcome."

Chapter 4

Mrs. Kantavoska (as the woman was actually called) lived on the farm with her husband and three children. In addition, they had a farmhand and two hired girls. Three days ago she had received word that a thirteen-year-old girl would probably be arriving within the next few days. If they took her in, they wouldn't be obliged to quarter anyone else in their house. Mrs. Kantavoska had readily agreed, and she now assumed that this was the girl.

The Kantavoskas had difficulty explaining things to Paula. However much she tried, Paula simply couldn't understand what they expected her to do. During the first two weeks, she could barely choke down the food, but since hunger makes even the oddest things taste good, she eventually got used to it, and after a while she rolled up her sleeves and, by imitating the others, was able to do the washing and mending.

So Paula's life went on, and after six months she could understand quite a bit of Russian. By the time another six months had gone by, she could understand almost everything and occasionally joined in the conversation, though it wasn't easy. The Kantavoskas didn't see Paula's bad side, since she was much too smart to pull any of her shenanigans here, and there was no point in making her life in Russia miserable as well. She did her chores, and since she wasn't as clumsy as she had pretended to be at home, she gradually became part of the family.

Chapter 5

After two years with the Kantavoskas, Paula was asked if she wanted to learn how to read and write in Russian. She eagerly accepted the offer, and from then on she and a neighbor girl went three times a week to reading and writing class. She made rapid progress, and after about twelve weeks she was able to read Russian. Both Paula and the other girl were also given permission to learn how to dance. Before long, you could find her every evening in a dance hall, dancing polkas and mazurkas for a few pennies a night. She gave half of her earnings to Mother Kantavoska and slipped the other half into her own pocket, since she had long been meaning to find a way to leave the country.

Meanwhile, the war had come to an end, though in all that time she had not heard a word from her parents.

Chapter 6

She was now nearly sixteen, poorly educated and aware of the fact that, by Western standards, she was quite ignorant. So she threw herself into her dancing, and before long she had saved enough money to buy a train ticket from Minsk (for that was the area she was in) to Warsaw. "If I can just get to Warsaw," she thought, "the Red Cross is bound to send me the rest of the way."

No sooner said than done. One morning, when she was supposedly going to class, she tied her accumulated possessions into a bundle and slipped away. As she had expected, the walk from the Kantavoskas' farm to Minsk was far from easy. She got a ride in a wagon for a few hours, but that still left several hours on foot.

She arrived in Minsk at dusk, totally exhausted. She went directly to the station and asked about the trains to Warsaw, but to her dismay, she was told that the first train wasn't due to leave until noon the next day. She pleaded with them to let her speak to the stationmaster, and when he appeared, she begged him for permission to sleep in the station that night. This was allowed, and she was so tired that she fell asleep at once. She awoke at dawn, stiff from head to toe, wondering where she was, but it all came back to her much too quickly when her stomach began to growl. That was something Paula had not anticipated. There was a nice girl at the station buffet, and after hearing Paula's open-hearted tale, she nicely gave her, at no charge, a real Russian bread roll. She spent the morning chatting with the waitress and boarded the train to Warsaw at noon, greatly cheered and in the highest of hopes.

Chapter 7

When she arrived in Warsaw, she asked the stationmaster for directions, then walked straight to the house of the Red Cross nurses. She stayed there longer than she'd expected, since none of the nurses knew what to do with her. They didn't have any addresses or lists of missing persons, and as Paula didn't have a penny to her name, they couldn't put her on a train. Nor could they let her starve to death. However, after a while the nurses decided, thank goodness, to pay for her trip to Berlin out of their own pockets, since Paula had told them that once she was in Berlin she'd be able to find her way to her parents' house.

The nurses bade her an affectionate farewell and once again Paula boarded the train. At the next station a nice young man entered her compartment and soon struck up a conversation with the gutsy-looking girl. For the rest of the trip, Paula was to be found in the company of the handsome young soldier, and when they arrived in Berlin, the two of them arranged to meet again soon.

Paula set off at a brisk pace and before long she had reached her parents' house, which turned out to be empty and deserted. It had never occurred to her that her parents might have moved. What was she to do? Once more she found the Red Cross and told them her story in her halting German, and once more she was taken in and cared for, though her stay was limited to a maximum of fourteen days.

All she found out about her parents was that her mother had left Berlin to look for work elsewhere and that her father had been drafted in the last year of the war and was now lying wounded in a hospital somewhere.

She went straight out to look for some kind of household job, and when she found one, she hurried over to see Erich, the handsome young man. With his help, she was hired for three nights a week in a cabaret. And so her Russian dancing came in useful again.

Chapter 8

Paula had been working for some time when the cabaret announced one evening that in two weeks' time it was going to hold a big dance show, exclusively for the convalescent soldiers who had recently been discharged from various hospitals. On this special night, Paula was to have a big part in the performance. There were lots of rehearsals, and when she got home late at night, she was so tired that she could barely drag herself out of bed at seven o'clock the next morning. Her one and only source of comfort in this period was Erich. Their friendship had grown so much that Paula no longer knew how she could ever manage without him. When the big night finally arrived, Paula had stage fright for the first time in her life. Dancing for a roomful of men was decidedly unnerving. Still, all she could do was try, and with the thought of the extra money she'd earn, she was able to keep on going.

The evening went well, and afterward Paula joined Erich in the lobby. All of a sudden she froze, because not far from her, talking to another soldier, was her father. With a cry of joy, she rushed over and threw herself in his arms. Her father, who had grown quite old, looked amazed, since he hadn't recognized his daughter, either on or off stage. She actually had to introduce herself!

Chapter 9

A week later Paula could be seen entering the train station in Frankfurt arm-in-arm with her father. They were welcomed by her deeply moved mother, who after all that time had almost given up hoping for her daughter's return.

After she'd told her mother the whole story, her father jokingly asked her if she'd like to hop on a plane so that she could fly back to Russia!

Bear in mind that this story takes place during the 1914–1918 war, when the Germans won the Russian campaign.

Delusions of Stardom

Friday, December 24, 1943

My answer to Mrs. van Daan, who's forever asking me why I don't want to be a movie star.

I was seventeen, a pretty young girl with curly black hair, mischievous eyes and . . . lots of ideals and illusions. I was sure that someday, somehow, my name would be on everyone's lips, my picture in many a starry-eyed teenager's photo album.

Exactly how I'd become a celebrity or what direction my career would take was of little concern to me. When I was fourteen, I used to think, "All in good time," and now that I'm seventeen, I still think that. My parents suspected almost nothing of my plans and I was smart enough to keep them to myself, since I had the feeling that if I ever got a chance to be famous they wouldn't like it and that, at least to start with, I'd be better off on my own.

You mustn't think that I took my daydreams seriously or that I thought of nothing but fame. On the contrary, I studied as hard as ever and always had my nose in a book—for my own pleasure.

At the age of fifteen, I passed my exams and switched from a three-year high school to a language class. In the mornings I went to school and in the afternoons I did my homework and played tennis.

One day (it was autumn), I was at home, cleaning out my junk closet, which was filled with boxes of every shape and kind, when I came across a shoebox marked "Movie Stars," in great big letters. The moment I laid eyes on it I remembered that I'd promised my parents to throw it out and that I'd probably tucked it away where nobody could find it.

Curious, I lifted the lid, took out those neat little bundles and started removing the rubber bands. I was so engrossed in those made-up faces that I couldn't stop, and two hours later, when someone tapped me on the shoulder, I jumped and looked up from where I was sitting on the floor, surrounded by a mound of clippings and boxes. They were stacked so high that I could barely step over them to go have a cup of tea.

Later, when I was clearing up the mess, I put the movie-star box to one side. That evening, as I was poring over it again, I came across something that I couldn't get out of my mind: an envelope filled with pictures, big and small, of the Lane family, whose three daughters, I read, were movie stars. I also found the girls' address, so . . . I picked up a pen and paper and began writing a letter in English to Priscilla Lane, the youngest of the three daughters.

Without telling a soul, I mailed this little epistle. In it, I wrote that I'd love to have pictures of Priscilla and her sisters and asked her to please answer my letter since I took a keen interest in her entire family.

I waited for more than two months, and though I didn't want to admit it to myself, I'd actually lost hope of ever getting an answer. It was hardly surprising, since I realized that if the Lane sisters had to write long letters to all their fans and send each of them a photograph, they'd find themselves, after only a few weeks, doing nothing all day but answering their correspondence.

But then one morning . . . just when I'd stopped expecting a reply, my father handed me an envelope addressed to "Miss Anne Franklin," which I eagerly ripped open. My family was curious to know what it was, so, after telling them about my letter, I read Priscilla's answer out loud.

She wrote that she couldn't send me any pictures without first knowing more about me, but that she'd be prepared to write back if I would tell her more about myself and my family. I replied, in all truth, that I was much more interested in her as a person than as an actress. I wanted to know if she went out in the evening, if Rosemary made as many movies as she did, etc., etc. Much later, she gave me permission to call her by her nickname, Pat. Apparently Priscilla was so taken with my "writing style," as she put it, that she was more than happy to send me long letters in return.

Since our correspondence was entirely in English, my parents could hardly object; after all, it was excellent practice for me. In the letters that followed, Priscilla told me that she spent most of her days at the studios, and outlined her daily schedule. She corrected my mistakes and mailed the letters back to me, though she wanted me to return them. In the meantime, she also sent a series of pictures.

Though Priscilla was already twenty years old, she was neither engaged nor married; still, it didn't bother me in the least, and I was terribly proud of my movie-star friend.

And so it went throughout the winter. Then one day, in late spring, I received a letter from the Lanes, in which Priscilla asked me if I'd like to fly to California and stay with her for two months during the summer. I jumped up and down so hard I nearly hit the ceiling, but I hadn't counted on my parents' numerous objections: I couldn't travel on my own, I couldn't possibly accept such an invitation, I didn't have enough clothes, I couldn't stay away that long . . . and all the other objections that worried parents have when it comes to their offspring. But I had my heart set on going to America, and I was determined to go.

I wrote and told Priscilla of all these objections, and she came up with a solution to every one. In the first place, I wouldn't have to travel on my own, since Priscilla's companion would be coming to The Hague for four weeks to visit her relatives and I could fly back with her. Some kind of escort could surely be arranged for the return trip.

Naturally I'd get to see a lot of California. But my parents still objected to the plan, this time on the grounds that they didn't know the family, and that I might feel out of place . . .

I was furious. It was as though they begrudged me the opportunity of a lifetime. Priscilla was being incredibly nice and considerate, and the upshot of all the fuss was that, after a personal letter from Mrs. Lane, the decision was finally handed down in my favor.

I studied hard during May and June. When Priscilla wrote that her companion would be arriving in Amsterdam on July 18, my preparations for the big trip began in earnest.

On the eighteenth, Father and I went to the station to meet her. Priscilla had sent me a picture, so I picked her out almost immediately in the crowd. Miss Kalwood was a small woman with graying blond hair who talked a lot and spoke incredibly fast, but she looked quite pleasant and nice.

Father, who had been in America and spoke excellent English, talked to Miss Kalwood, and every once in a while I put in a word or two.

We had agreed that Miss Kalwood would stay at our house for a week before going back, and the week simply flew by. Even before the first day was over she and I had become friends. I was so excited on July 25 that I couldn't swallow a single bite of breakfast.

Miss Kalwood, on the other hand, was as cool as a cucumber. But then, this wasn't her first flight. The entire family went to Schiphol Airport to see us off. At last . . . at long last, my trip to America had begun.

We flew for nearly five days. On the evening of the fifth day, we arrived at a place not far from Hollywood. Priscilla and her sister Rosemary, who is one year older, met us at the airport. I was rather tired from the journey, so we quickly drove to a nearby hotel.

The next morning, we had a leisurely breakfast before getting back in the car, which Rosemary herself drove.

We reached the Lanes' house in just over three hours, and I was given a warm welcome. Mrs. Lane showed me to an adorable room with a balcony, which was to be mine for the next two months.

It was not difficult to feel at ease in the hospitable Lane home, where there was a constant buzz of activity and fun, where you stumbled over any number of cats with every step you took, where the three famous stars did more to help their mother than an ordinary teenager like me had ever done at home and where there was so much to see. I quickly got used to speaking a foreign language, especially since I had known a bit of English before I came.

Priscilla was free during the first two weeks of my vacation and showed me around much of the surrounding area. Almost every day we went to the beach, and little by little I got to know people whose names I'd heard so often. Madge Bellamy was one of Priscilla's best friends, and she frequently went with us on our sightseeing trips.

People who knew Priscilla would never have guessed that she was so much older than I was. She and I were simply friends. After the first two weeks, Priscilla went back to work at Warner Bros. and they let me go to the studio too, which was sheer bliss. I went with her to her dressing room and stayed there while she was busy with the takes.

She finished early on the first day, so she took me on a tour of the studio. "Hey, Anne," she suddenly said. "I've got a great idea. Tomorrow morning, why don't you go down to one of those casting offices, where all the beautiful girls go, and see if they've got anything for you. Just for fun, of course!"

"Oh, I'd like that," I replied, and the next day I really did go to a casting office. It was unbelievably busy, with a long line of girls waiting outside the door. I joined the queue,* and after half an hour found myself on the other side of the door. Though I'd made it inside, it still wasn't my turn; there were at least twenty-five girls ahead of me. So I waited again, for an hour or two, until my turn came.

A bell rang, and I bravely stepped inside the office, where a middle-aged man was seated behind a desk. His greeting was fairly abrupt. He asked my name and address and was very surprised to hear that I was staying at the Lanes'. When the questions were over, he looked me up and down again and said, "Are you sure you want to be a movie star?"

"Yes, sir, very much, if you think I have the talent," I replied.

He pressed a buzzer and immediately a smartly dressed girl came in. She motioned for me to follow her. She opened a door, and for a moment all I could do was blink, since the room was filled with a blinding bright light.

A young man behind a very intricate camera greeted me in a friendlier way than the older man in the office, and told me to sit on a tall stool. He took a few pictures, then rang for the girl, who led me back to the "old" guy. He promised to let me know whether or not they wanted me. Delighted, I turned down the road to the Lanes' house.

A week went by before I heard from Mr. Harwich (Priscilla had told me his name). He wrote that the pic-

---

*Anne's word.

tures looked quite good and that he would see me the following day at three o'clock.

This time I was ushered in ahead of the others because I had been sent for. Harwich asked me if I'd like to model for a company that made tennis rackets. The job was just for one week. After hearing what the pay was, I said yes. A call was made to the tennis manufacturer, and I met him the same afternoon.

The next day I reported to a photo studio, which I was supposed to go to every day for a week. I had to change clothes continually, stand here, sit there, keep a smile plastered on my face, parade up and down, change again, look angelic and redo my makeup for the umpteenth time. I was so exhausted every evening that I had to drag myself to bed. After three days, it was all I could do to squeeze out a smile. But . . . I felt I had to keep my agreement with the manufacturer.

On the evening of the fourth day, I was so pale when I arrived at the Lanes' that Mrs. Lane forbade me to do another day's modeling. She even called the tennis manufacturer and had him cancel the contract.

I thanked her from the bottom of my heart.

After that I was free to enjoy the rest of my unforgettable vacation, and now that I had seen the life of the stars up close, I was cured once and for all of my delusions of fame.

Katrien

Friday, February 11, 1944

Katrien was sitting on a boulder that lay in the sun in front of the farm. She was thinking, thinking very hard. Katrien was one of those quiet girls who become [blank]* in later years, because they're always thinking.

What the little girl in the pinafore was thinking about only she could say, because she never told her thoughts to anyone. She was much too quiet and withdrawn for that.

She didn't have a single girlfriend and probably wouldn't find it easy to make one. Her mother thought she was a strange child, and unfortunately Katrien could sense her disapproval. Her father, the farmer, was far too busy to concern himself with his only daughter. So Katrien was always by herself. She didn't mind being on her own; she thought it was normal and was happy to let it go at that.

On this hot summer day, however, she looked out over the wheat fields and sighed deeply. How fun it would be to be able to play with the girls over there. Look at them running and laughing and having a good time!

---

*A word is missing in the original manuscript.

The girls started coming closer and closer . . . Do you suppose they were coming over to where she was sitting? Oh, how awful, they were laughing at her. She could clearly hear them calling her name, the nickname she hated so much, the one she heard them whispering behind her back: Katrien the Lazy Bean. Oh, she felt so miserable. If only she could run into the house, but then they'd laugh at her even more.

Poor little girl. This can't be the first time you've felt so lonely, or envied girls who are even poorer than you.

"Katrien, Katrien, come in, it's time to eat!" She sighed one last time and got up slowly to obey her mother's call.

"Oh, she's got her happy face on again! Our little girl is just as cheerful as can be!" her mother exclaimed as Katrien shuffled into the room even slower and sadder than usual.

"Can't you even answer?" the woman snapped. She wasn't aware of how unfriendly her voice sounded, but her daughter wasn't at all like the cheerful, lively girl she longed to have.

"Yes, Mother." Her reply was nearly inaudible.

"You're a fine one to talk. You've been gone all morning and haven't done a single bit of work. Where have you been?"

"Out front."

There seemed to be a giant lump in Katrien's throat, but her mother, misinterpreting the child's bashfulness and now justifiably curious about what her daughter had been up to all morning, asked her again: "I want to know where you've been, and I expect a clear answer this time.

Is that understood? You're such a lazy little thing and I hate laziness!"

Upon hearing the word that reminded her of her detested nickname, Katrien lost control of herself and burst into tears.

"Now what's the matter? You're such a scaredy-cat. Can't you tell me where you've been, or is that such a big secret?"

The poor child was crying so hard she couldn't answer. Suddenly she stood up, knocking over her chair, and, sobbing, raced out of the room and up to the attic, where she slumped down on a pile of gunny sacks in the corner and quietly cried her eyes out.

Her mother shrugged and cleared the table. She wasn't surprised at her daughter's behavior. This wasn't the first time she'd seen her in one of these "crazy" moods. It was best to leave the child alone. After all, you couldn't get a word out of her when she was like this, and she was liable to break into tears at the drop of a hat. What kind of behavior was that for a twelve-year-old farm girl?

Upstairs in the attic, Katrien had calmed down and was thinking again. In a moment she'd go back down and tell her mother that she'd simply been sitting on the boulder, and offer to finish all her chores this afternoon. Then her mother would see that she didn't mind working hard, and if she asked her why she'd been sitting on her duff all morning, she'd tell her that she needed to have a good think. This evening, when she went to the village to deliver the eggs, she'd buy her mother a new thimble, a nice shiny silver thimble. She had just enough money. Then Mother would see that she wasn't a Lazy Bean after all.

Her train of thought came to a brief halt. Oh, dear, how was she ever going to get rid of that dreadful nickname? Wait, she had an idea. With the money that was bound to be left over after she bought the thimble, she could buy a big bag of candy—the red, sticky kind the other farm kids were so fond of—and tomorrow she would give them to the teacher, who could pass them out to all the girls. Then they'd be sure to like her and ask her to play with them, and then they'd see that she was good at games too, and never again would she be called anything but Katrien.

Still feeling a bit hesitant, she stood up and tiptoed down the stairs. In the hall, she ran into her mother, who said, "Got over your little tantrum, have you?," so that she no longer felt up to telling her where she'd been. Instead, she hurried past so she could get the windows washed before it got dark.

Just before sundown Katrien set off at a fast pace with a basket of eggs on her arm. After half an hour, she reached her first customer, already waiting in the doorway with a porcelain bowl in her hand.

"I'll take a dozen eggs, dear," the woman said kindly.

Katrien counted them out, said goodbye and went on her way; three-quarters of an hour later the basket was empty and Katrien was entering a little store that sold all kinds of goods. With a pretty thimble and a bag of candy tucked in her basket, she began the return journey. She was halfway home when she saw two of the girls who had laughed at her this morning coming toward her. Bravely overcoming the desire to hide, she continued down the road, though her heart was pounding wildly.

"Hey, there's Lazy Bean. That crazy Lazy Bean."

Katrien's heart sank. In desperation, knowing she had to do something, she took the candy out of her basket and held it out to the girls. One of them snatched the bag and ran away. The other one raced after her, stopping only to stick out her tongue before disappearing around a bend in the road.

Helpless, heartbroken and lonely, Katrien sank into the grass at the side of the road and wept—wept until she had no more tears. Darkness had already set in by the time she picked up the overturned basket and headed home. From somewhere in the grass came the gleam of a silver thimble . . .

Sundays

❧

Sunday, February 20, 1944

What happens in other people's houses during the rest of
the week happens here in the Annex on Sundays. While
other people put on their best clothes and go strolling in
the sun, we scrub, sweep and do the laundry.

Eight o'clock: Though the rest of us prefer to sleep in,
Dussel gets up at eight. He goes to the bathroom, then
downstairs, then up again and then to the bathroom,
where he devotes a whole hour to washing himself.

Nine-thirty: The stoves are lit, the blackout screen is
taken down and Mr. van Daan heads for the bathroom.
One of my Sunday morning ordeals is having to lie in bed
and look at Dussel's back when he's praying. I know it
sounds strange, but a praying Dussel is a terrible sight to
behold. It's not that he cries or gets sentimental, not at all,
but he does spend a quarter of an hour—an entire fifteen
minutes—rocking from his toes to his heels. Back and
forth, back and forth. It goes on forever, and if I don't shut
my eyes tight, my head starts to spin.

Ten-fifteen: The van Daans whistle; the bathroom's free.
In the Frank family quarters, the first sleepy faces are

beginning to emerge from their pillows. Then everything happens fast, fast, fast. Margot and I take turns doing the laundry. Since it's quite cold downstairs, we put on pants and head scarves. Meanwhile, Father is busy in the bathroom. Either Margot or I have a turn in the bathroom at eleven, and then all is clean.

Eleven-thirty: Breakfast. I won't dwell on this, since there's enough talk about food without my bringing the subject up as well.

Twelve-fifteen: We each go our own separate ways. Father, clad in overalls, gets down on his hands and knees and brushes the rug so vigorously that the room is enveloped in a cloud of dust. Mr. Dussel makes the beds (all wrong, of course), always whistling the same Beethoven violin concerto as he goes about his work. Mother can be heard shuffling around the attic as she hangs up the washing.

Mr. van Daan puts on his hat and disappears into the lower regions, usually followed by Peter and Mouschi. Mrs. van D. dons a long apron, a black wool jacket and overshoes, winds a red wool scarf around her head, scoops up a bundle of dirty laundry and, with a well-rehearsed washerwoman's nod, heads downstairs.

Margot and I do the dishes and straighten up the room.

Twelve forty-five: When all the dishes have been dried and only the pots and pans are left, I go downstairs to dust and, if I washed myself this morning, to clean the sink.

One: News.

One-fifteen: Time for one of us to wash our hair or get a haircut. Next, all of us are busy peeling potatoes, hanging up the laundry, scrubbing the landing, scouring the bathroom, etc., etc.

Two: After the Wehrmacht news, we wait for the music program and the coffee, so there's a moment of peace. Can anyone tell me why the adults around here need so much sleep? By eleven A.M. several of them are already yawning, and they spend half their time moaning, "Oh, if only I could grab half an hour of sleep!"

It's no fun seeing nothing but sleepy faces wherever you go between two and four in the afternoon: Dussel in our room, Mother and Father next door and the van Daans upstairs, sharing a bed during the daytime. Still, I can't do a blessed thing about it. Perhaps I'll understand it one day when I'm as old as they are.

Anyway, naptime is stretched out even longer on Sundays. There's no point in showing yourself upstairs before four thirty or five, since they're all still in the Land of Nod.

Late afternoons are the same as on weekdays, except for the concert hour from six to seven.

When dinner's over and the dishes are done, I'm beside myself with joy because another Sunday is over.

The Flower Girl

Sunday, February 20, 1944

At seven-thirty every morning the door of a cottage on the outskirts of the village swings open and out comes a rather small girl with a basket full of flowers on each arm. Once she's shut the door behind her, she adjusts the two baskets and sets off.

Every person in the village who sees her go by and receives one of her friendly nods can't help feeling sorry for her, and every day they think the same thing: "It's too long and difficult a walk for a twelve-year-old child." But the little girl doesn't know what the villagers are thinking, so as quickly and as cheerfully as she can she walks on . . . and on.

It's really a very long way to the city: at least two and a half hours of steady walking. And two heavy baskets don't make it any easier. By the time she's finally walking down the city sidewalks, she's exhausted. The prospect of being able to sit down soon and rest is all that keeps her going. But she's a plucky little thing, and she doesn't slow down until she reaches her spot in the market. Then she sits down and waits . . . and waits . . .

Sometimes she has to wait all day, since not many people want to buy what the poor little flower girl is selling. More than once Krista has had to go back home with her baskets half full.

But today is different. It's Wednesday, and unusually busy at the market. The women next to her are loudly hawking their wares, and all around her she hears shrill and angry voices.

The passersby can barely hear Krista, for the hustle and bustle of the market nearly drowns out her high little voice. But all day long she keeps calling out, "Beautiful flowers, ten cents a bunch! Buy my beautiful flowers!" And when the people who've finished their shopping take a look into those full baskets, they end up giving Krista ten cents just to have one of her beautifully arranged bouquets.

Every day at twelve o'clock, Krista gets up from her chair and walks over to the other side of the market, where the owner of the coffee stand gives her a free cup of steaming hot coffee with plenty of sugar. Krista saves her prettiest bunch of flowers for him.

Then she returns to her chair and starts hawking her wares again. At last, when it's three-thirty, she gets up, collects her baskets and heads back to her village. She walks more slowly now than in the morning. Krista is tired, terribly tired.

This time the trip takes three hours, so that it's six-thirty before she finally reaches the door of her cramped old cottage. Inside, everything is just as she left it in the morning: cold, lonely and bleak. Her sister, who shares the cottage with her, works in the village from early in the morning to late at night.

Krista can't allow herself a moment's rest. As soon as she gets home, she starts peeling potatoes and boiling vegetables. Only when her sister arrives home at seven-thirty does she finally get to sit down and eat her meager meal.

At eight o'clock the door of the cottage swings open again and out comes the little girl with the two big baskets on her arms. This time her steps take her to the meadows and fields surrounding the cottage. She doesn't walk far, but leans over in the grass and begins to pick the flowers—all sorts of flowers, big ones, small ones, colors of every kind—into her baskets they go, and though the sun has nearly gone down, the little girl is still sitting in the grass, picking flower after flower.

At last she's through, her baskets are full. In the meantime the sun has set. Krista lies down in the grass, with her hands cupped behind her head and her eyes open, and looks at what's left of the pale-blue sky.

This is the finest fifteen minutes of her day. You mustn't think that the little flower girl, who's worked so hard, is unhappy. She's never unhappy, and as long as she has these few moments every day, she never will be.

There in the meadow, among the flowers and the grass, beneath the wide-open sky, Krista is content. Gone is her exhaustion, gone are the market and the people; she thinks and dreams only of the present. If only she can have this every day, a whole fifteen minutes of doing nothing, alone with God and nature.

My First Interview

❦

Imagine what would happen if the subject of my first interview knew he was going to be used as material! He would no doubt turn red and say, "Me? What's there to interview?"

I won't keep you in suspense any longer: Peter is my subject. I'll also tell you how the idea came to me! I was thinking of interviewing someone, and since I've written about every person in this house over and over again, I suddenly thought of Peter, who's always in the background, and—like Margot—almost never does anything that can give rise to dissatisfaction or quarrels.

Early in the evening, when you knock on his door and hear his soft-spoken "Come in," you can be sure that when you open the door, he'll be looking at you through the steps of the ladder to the attic, and that most of the time he'll utter an inviting "So there you are!"

His room is actually a . . . hmm, I'm not sure what it is. I think it's a kind of landing going up to the attic. It's very small, very dark and very damp, but . . . he's managed to turn it into a real room.

When he's sitting to the left of the ladder, there's only about three feet between it and the wall. This is where he has his table, which is usually strewn with books like ours is (the steps also get the overflow), and a chair. On the other side of the ladder is his bicycle, suspended from the ceiling. This now useless form of transportation has been wrapped in packing paper, and a long extension cord dangles merrily from one of the pedals. To add the finishing touch to the interviewee's work space, the lightbulb above his head has been covered with the latest trend in lampshades: cardboard decorated with strips of paper.

From where I'm standing in the doorway, I look to the opposite side of the room. Against the wall, i.e., across from Peter, behind the table, there's a divan with a flowery blue spread; the bedding has been tucked behind the backrest. There's a lamp hanging above it, much like the one two feet away, as well as a hand mirror, and a bit farther away, a bookcase filled from top to bottom with books that have been covered—with a boy's typical disregard of elegance—with packing paper. To spruce things up even more (or because the owner has no other place to put it), there's also a toolbox, where you're sure to find whatever you're looking for. Though it admittedly happened quite a while ago, I once found my favorite knife, which had long been missing, in the bottom of this very toolbox, and it wasn't the first thing to find its way there.

Next to the bookcase is a wooden shelf, covered with paper that used to be white. Actually, this shelf was supposed to be for milk bottles and other kitchen items. But the youthful occupant's treasury of books has expanded so rapidly that the shelf has been taken over by these learned tomes, and the various milk bottles have been relegated to the floor.

The third wall also has a small cupboard (a former cherry crate), where you can find a delightful collection of such things as a shaving brush, a razor, tape, laxatives, etc., etc. Beside it is the crowning glory of the van Daan family's ingenuity: a closet made almost entirely out of cardboard, held together by only two or three support posts made of stronger material. This closet, which is filled with suits, coats, shoes, socks and so forth, has a really lovely curtain hanging in front of it, which Peter finally managed to lay hold of after weeks of begging his mother. So much stuff is piled on top of the closet that I've never figured out exactly what's there.

The rugs of Mr. van Daan Junior are also worthy of note. Not only because his room has two large genuine Persian carpets and one small one, but because the colors are so striking that everyone who enters the room notices them right away. So the floorboards, which have to be negotiated with care since they're rather loose and uneven, are adorned with these precious rugs.

Two of the walls have been covered in green burlap, while the other two have been lavishly plastered with movie stars—some beautiful, others less so—and advertisements. You need to overlook the grease and burn marks, since, after one and a half years of living with so much junk, things are bound to get dirty.

The attic, hardly the height of comfort either, is like all the others around here, with old-fashioned beams, and since the loft leaks down via the attic into Peter's room, several sheets of cardboard have been put up to keep out the rain. The many water stains show that it's not the least bit effective.

I think I've been around the entire room now and have only forgotten the two chairs: number one is a brown chair with a perforated seat, and number two is an old white kitchen chair. Peter wanted to repaint it last year, but noticed when he was scraping off the old layer that it wasn't such a good idea. So now the chair, with its partially stripped paint, its one and only rung (the other was used as a poker) and its more-black-than-white color scheme, is not exactly presentable. But as I've already said, the room is dark, so the chair hardly sticks out. The door to the kitchen is festooned with aprons, and there are also a few hooks for the dust cloths and cleaning brush.

Now that Peter's room has been dealt with, you should have no trouble picking out every item in it, except for the chief occupant himself, Peter. So I'd like to complete my assignment by turning to the owner of the glorious items catalogued above.

In Peter's case, there's a big difference between his weekday clothes and his Sunday best. On weekdays he wears overalls. In fact, you can say without hesitation that he and his overalls are inseparable, since he won't allow them to be washed very often. The only reason I can think of is that he's afraid his beloved garment will fall to pieces in the wash and have to be thrown out. At any rate, it was washed recently, which is how you can tell it's blue. He also has a blue kerchief (another inseparable item) knotted around his neck, a thick brown leather belt around his waist, and white wool socks, so that whether it's a Monday, a Tuesday or any other day of the week, you can recognize Peter right away. On Sundays, however, his outfit undergoes a radical change. A nice suit, a nice pair of shoes, a shirt, a tie—well, there's no need for me to list the rest, since we all know what decent clothes look like.

So much for his appearance. My opinion of Peter himself has changed drastically of late. I used to think he was stupid and boring. Now I think he's neither of these, and everyone will agree when I say that he's turned out to be quite nice.

I'm absolutely convinced that he's honest and generous. He's always been modest and helpful, but I have the feeling that he's much more sensitive than people realize or would ever suspect.

One thing he's fond of and which I absolutely mustn't forget is the cats. There's nothing he wouldn't do for Mouschi or Boche, and I think they compensate quite a lot for the love he needs but doesn't get.

He isn't afraid either—quite the opposite, in fact, without being cocky like other boys his age. Nor is he the least bit stupid. In particular, I think he has an excellent memory.

I hardly need to tell you that he's handsome, since that's obvious to everyone who knows him. He has terrific hair—thick, brown and curly—and bluish-gray eyes. As for his other features . . . well, describing faces has always been my weak point, so when the war's over I'll paste a picture of him in this book, along with pictures of the rest of us in hiding here, so that I won't have to describe him further with my pen.

The Den of Iniquity

Tuesday, February 22, 1944

Don't be shocked—I'm not planning to give examples of the above title. I only chose it because I ran across the phrase yesterday in a magazine that I was reading.

No doubt you're wondering what it referred to, so I'll explain. The "den of iniquity" was used in the magazine (*Cinema & Theater*, no. 8) to refer to the use of nude models, which the reviewer apparently thought was indecent. Now, it's certainly not my intention to argue that he's wrong, but in my opinion Dutch people tend to frown on scanty dress.

This is known as prudishness. On the one hand, it can be good. On the other hand, if children are raised to think that even the slightest bit of bare skin is indecent, after a certain amount of time adolescents are bound to wonder, "Are they all stark raving mad?"

And I couldn't agree more. Modesty and prudishness can be taken too far, which is certainly the case in the Netherlands. Actually, it's quite paradoxical—just mention the word "naked," and everyone will stare at you as if you're the most depraved person in the world.

Don't think I'm like those people who long for a return to the days of primitive societies, when everyone was walking around in animal skins. Not at all. Still, it would be more natural if we were a bit freer, a bit more casual.

And now I have a question for you. "Do you also put clothes on the flowers you've picked and refuse to talk about their delicate parts?"

I don't think there's a very big difference between people and nature, and since we're also part of nature, why should we be ashamed of the way nature made us?

The Guardian Angel

Tuesday, February 22, 1944

Once upon a time there were two people, an old woman and her granddaughter, who lived for many years at the edge of a great big forest. The little girl's parents had died when she was very young, and her grandmother had always looked after her. Their cottage was lonely and isolated, but they didn't think so, and the two of them were always happy and content together.

One morning the old woman couldn't get out of bed. She was in great pain. Her granddaughter was fourteen years old at the time, and she took care of her grandma as well as she knew how. Five days went by, then the grandmother died, leaving the girl all alone in the cottage. She knew almost no one, nor did she want to ask a stranger to bury her grandmother, so she dug a deep grave under an old tree in the forest, and there she laid her grandma to rest.

When the poor child came home again, she felt sad and utterly alone. She lay down on her bed and wept. She stayed in bed for the rest of the day, only getting up in the evening to have a bite to eat.

And so it went day after day. The poor child no longer

felt like doing anything but mourning the loss of her dear sweet grandma. Then something happened that changed her life completely from one day to the next.

It was night and the girl was asleep. Suddenly her grandmother was standing before her—dressed all in white, with her white hair down around her shoulders, and a tiny lamp in her hand. The girl looked up from her bed and waited for her grandmother to speak.

"My dear little girl," the grandmother began. "I've been watching you every day for the last four weeks. All you've done is cry and sleep. That's not right. So I've come to tell you that you need to keep busy, to get back to your weaving and to clean our cottage, and also to put on pretty clothes again!

"You mustn't think that I'll stop looking after you now that I'm dead. I'm in Heaven, watching you from up above. I've become your guardian angel, and I'll always be at your side, just like I used to be. Go back to your work, my darling, and don't ever forget that Grandma is with you!"

The grandmother faded away and the girl went on sleeping. However, when she woke up the next morning, she remembered her grandmother's words and suddenly felt happy because she was no longer alone. She busied herself again, going to the market to sell her weaving, and she always followed her grandma's advice.

Later, many years later, she was again no longer alone in the world, because she married a fine miller. She thanked her grandma for not having left her. And though she had a husband to keep her company now, she knew that her guardian angel would be with her until the day she died.

Happiness

Sunday, March 12, 1944

Before I begin with the actual story, I need to give you a brief rundown of my life so far.

I no longer have a mother (in fact I never knew her), and my father has little time for me. My mother died when I was two. My father farmed me out to a kindly couple who kept me for five years. When I was seven, I was sent to a kind of boarding school, where I stayed until I was fourteen. Luckily, I was allowed to leave then, and Father took me in. The two of us are living in a rooming house now and I'm attending the Lyceum. Everything in my life was going normally until . . . well, until Jacques came along.

I met Jacques when he and his parents moved into the rooming house. We ran into each other a few times on the stairs, then in the park, and after that we went for several walks in the woods together.

I thought he was a nice, easygoing type from the start. A bit shy and on the quiet side, but that's exactly what attracted me to him in the first place. We gradually began going places together, and now he often comes to my room, or I go to his.

Before I met Jacques, I'd never gotten to know a boy really well. So I was also surprised to find that he wasn't a braggart or a show-off like the boys in my class all seemed to be.

I started to think about Jacques after first giving quite a bit of thought to myself. I knew that his parents argued all the time, and I assumed that it bothered him, because one of the first things you notice about him is his love of peace and quiet.

I'm by myself a lot, and I often feel sad and lonely. It probably comes from missing my mother so much and from never having had a real friend I could tell everything to. Jacques is just the same—he's had only casual friends—and I had the feeling that he also needed to confide in someone. But I couldn't find an appropriate moment, so we continued to talk about trivial things.

One day, however, he came to my room, supposedly to deliver a message. I was sitting on the floor on a cushion, and looking up at the sky.

"Am I disturbing you?" he asked softly.

"Not at all," I replied, turning toward him. "Come and sit down. Do you also like to daydream sometimes?"

He went over to the window and leaned his forehead against the windowpane. "Yes," he replied. "I do a lot of daydreaming. Do you know what I call it? Gazing into world history."

Surprised, I looked at him. "That's a perfect description of it. I'll remember that."

"Yes," he said with that unusual smile of his, which always threw me for a loop, since I was never sure what he meant by it. We went back to talking about trivial matters, and after half an hour he left.

The next time he came to my room, I was sitting in the same spot and he went over to the window again. The weather was exceptionally beautiful that day—the sky was deep blue (we were up so high that we couldn't see any houses, or at any rate I couldn't from the floor), the bare branches of the chestnut tree in front of our house were covered with drops of dew that glinted in the sunlight as the branches swayed back and forth in the wind, seagulls and other birds flew past the window and chirping sounds were coming from every direction.

I don't know why, but neither of us could say another word. There we were together in one room, fairly close, yet we hardly noticed each other's presence. We just kept on gazing at the sky and talking to ourselves. I say "we," because I'm convinced that he was feeling the same and was just as reluctant as I was to break the silence.

After about fifteen minutes of this, he was the first to speak. "When you see that," he said, "it seems crazy for people to argue all the time. Everything else becomes unimportant. And yet I don't always feel this way!"

He looked at me, a little shyly, probably afraid I wouldn't understand what he meant, but I was overjoyed that he expected an answer from me and that I could finally reveal my thoughts to someone who understood. So I replied: "Do you know what I always think? That it's silly to argue with people you don't care about. It's different with people you do care about. You love them, so when they start an argument or do something to provoke a quarrel, it makes you feel more hurt than angry!"

"Do you think so too? But you don't get into very many arguments, do you?"

"No, but enough to know what they're like! Still, the worst thing of all is that most people are alone in the world!"

"What do you mean by that?" Jacques's eyes were now fixed on mine, but I decided to continue; perhaps I might be able to help him.

"I mean that most people, whether or not they're married, are lonely inside. They have no one to talk to about their thoughts and emotions. That's what I miss the most!"

All Jacques said was, "Me too." Then we went back to gazing at the sky for a while before he remarked, "Like you said, people who don't have anyone to talk to are missing out on a lot—a whole lot. It's knowing what I'm missing that often makes me feel so depressed."

"Well, you shouldn't. Not that you shouldn't feel depressed—after all, you can't help that, but you shouldn't feel miserable about something before it happens. Actually, what you're hoping to find when you're depressed is happiness. Even if you miss a lot because you have no one to talk to, once you've found your own inner happiness, you'll never lose it. I don't mean this in terms of material things, but in a spiritual sense. I believe that once your own inner happiness has been found, it might go underground for a while, but it will never be lost!"

"So how did you find your happiness?"

I got to my feet. "Come with me," I said. And I led him up to the attic, where there was a little storage room with a window. Our house was higher than most, so that, once we'd reached the attic and were looking out the window, we could see a large portion of the sky.

"Take a look," I said. "If you want to find inner happiness, go outside on a nice day with lots of sun and blue sky. Even if you stand at a window and look out over the city at the cloudless sky, like we're doing now, you'll eventually find happiness.

"I'll tell you how it happened to me. I was at boarding school. It had always been awful, but the older I got, the awfuler it got. On one of my free afternoons, I went for a walk on the heath by myself. I sat down and daydreamed for a while, and when I looked up, I noticed that it was an exceptionally beautiful day. I hadn't paid any attention to the weather up till then, because I'd been too wrapped up in my own troubles. But once I looked up and saw the beauty of my surroundings, that little voice inside me suddenly stopped itemizing the bad things. All I could do or think or feel was that it was beautiful, that it was the only real truth.

"I must have sat there for half an hour. When I finally got up to go back to that hateful school, I was no longer depressed. On the contrary, I felt that everything was good and beautiful just the way it was.

"Later on I understood that I had found my own inner happiness for the first time that afternoon. No matter what the circumstances are, that happiness will be with you always."

"Did it change you?" he quietly asked.

"Yes, in the sense that I felt a certain contentment. Not always, mind you. I moaned and groaned from time to time. But I was never downright depressed again, probably because I realized that sadness comes from feeling sorry for yourself and happiness from joy."

I stopped talking and he kept looking out the window,

apparently lost in thought, because he didn't say a word. Then he suddenly turned and looked at me. "I haven't found happiness yet, but I have found something else—a person who understands me!"

I knew what he meant, and from that moment on I was no longer alone.

Fear

❧

Saturday, March 25, 1944

It happened just as I was going through a terrible time. The war was raging all around us, and none of us knew if we'd live to see the next hour. My parents, brothers and sisters and I were living in the city, but we thought we might have to flee or be evacuated at any moment. The days were filled with the roar of guns and rifle shots, the nights with mysterious flashes and explosions that seemed to come from deep within the earth.

I can't describe it. I don't remember the details of those tumultuous days anymore, just the fact that I did nothing all day but feel frightened. My parents tried all sorts of things to calm me down, but none of them worked. I was scared inside and out. I couldn't eat or sleep, all I could do was tremble. That went on for a week, until the night that I remember as though it happened yesterday.

It was eight-thirty in the evening. The shooting had just died down a bit and I was dozing, fully dressed, on the divan when we were suddenly startled by two horrendous booms. We all leapt to our feet as if we'd been pricked with a pin, and went to stand in the hall. Even

Mother, who was normally so calm, looked pale. The booms were repeated at fairly regular intervals, then all of a sudden there was an enormous crash, followed by screams and the tinkle of broken glass, and I began running as fast as my legs would carry me. Bundled up in warm clothes with my knapsack on my back, I ran and ran, away from the horrible mass of flames.

I was surrounded on all sides by running and screaming people. The burning houses lit up the street and cast a fearful red glow on every object. I didn't think about my parents or brothers and sisters, only about myself, how I had to get farther and farther away. I didn't feel the exhaustion—my fear was stronger—or notice that I'd lost my knapsack. I just kept on running.

I have no idea how long I ran, spurred on by the image of burning houses, screaming and contorted faces, my fear of all that was happening. Suddenly I noticed that it had become quieter. I looked around, as if I'd just awakened from a dream, and saw nothing and no one. No fires, no bombs, no people.

I stopped running and looked more carefully. I was in a field of grass, the moon was shining and the stars were gleaming overhead, the weather was wonderful, the night was chilly but not cold. Hearing no more noise, I sank exhausted to the ground, spread out the blanket I was still carrying and lay down.

I gazed up at the sky and suddenly realized I was no longer afraid. On the contrary, I was quite calm. The odd thing was that I wasn't thinking of my family at all, nor did I long for them. I longed only for rest, and I soon fell fast asleep in the grass, beneath the starry sky.

* * *

When I awoke, the sun was just coming up. I instantly realized where I was when off in the distance the morning light revealed a row of familiar houses on the outskirts of the city. I rubbed my eyes and took a better look around. There wasn't a soul in sight. The dandelions and the clover leaves in the grass were my only company. I lay back down on the blanket and thought about what I should do next, but my thoughts kept wandering back to the wondrous feeling that had come over me in the night, when I had sat all by myself in the grass and not been afraid.

Later, I found my parents and we all went to live in another city. Now that the war has long been over, I know why my fear vanished beneath that spacious sky. You see, once I was alone with nature I realized, without actually being aware of it, that fear doesn't help, that it doesn't get you anywhere. Anyone who's as frightened as I was should look to nature and realize that God is much closer than most people think.

From that moment on, though countless bombs fell close by, I was never truly afraid again.

Give!*

❧

Sunday, March 26, 1944

Do any of those people in their warm and cozy living rooms have any idea what kind of life a beggar leads? Do any of those "good" and "kind" people ever wonder about the lives of so many of the children and adults around them? Granted, everyone has given a coin to a beggar at some time or another, though they usually just shove it into his hand and slam the door. And in most cases the generous donors think it's disgusting to touch that hand! Am I right or not? Then, afterwards, people are amazed that beggars are so shameless! Wouldn't you be shameless too if you were treated more like a dog than a human being?

It's terrible, really terrible, that people treat each other this way in a country like Holland, which claims to have such a good social system and so many decent, upstanding citizens. In the eyes of most of the well-to-do, a

---

*Based on one of Anne's grandmother's favorite sayings, which was often quoted by the Frank family: "People who give will never be poor."

beggar is an inferior being, somebody who's scruffy and unwashed, pushy and rude. But have they ever asked themselves how beggars got to be that way?

You should try comparing one of those beggar children with your own children! What's the difference? Yours are pretty and neat, the others are ugly and ragged! Is that all? Yes, that's all, that's the only difference. If you dressed one of those urchins in nice clothes and taught him good manners, there wouldn't be a whit of difference!

Everyone is born equal; we all come into the world helpless and innocent. We all breathe the same air, and many of us believe in the same God. And yet . . . and yet, to many people this one small difference is a huge one! It's huge because many people have never realized what the difference is, for if they had they would have discovered long ago that there's actually no difference at all!

Everyone is born equal; we will all die and shed our earthly glory. Riches, power and fame last for only a few short years. Why do we cling so desperately to these fleeting things? Why can't people who have more than enough for their own needs give the rest to their fellow human beings? Why should anyone have to have such a hard life for those few short years on earth?

But above all, a gift should never be flung in anyone's face—every person has a right to kindness. Why should you be nicer to a rich lady than to a poor one? Has anyone ever studied the difference in their characters?

Human greatness does not lie in wealth or power, but in character and goodness. People are just people, and all people have faults and shortcomings, but all of us are born with a basic goodness. If we were to start by adding to that goodness instead of stifling it, by giving poor people the feeling that they too are human beings, we wouldn't necessarily have to give money or material things, since not everyone has them to give.

Everything starts in small ways, so in this case you can begin in small ways too. On streetcars, for example, don't just offer your seat to rich mothers, think of the poor ones too. And say "excuse me" when you step on a poor person's toe, just as you say it to a rich one. It takes so little effort, yet it means so much. Why shouldn't you show a little kindness to those poor urchins who are already so deprived?

We all know that "example is better than precept." So set a good example, and it won't take long for others to follow. More and more people will become kind and generous, until finally no one will ever again look down on those without money.

Oh, if only we were already that far! If only Holland, then Europe, and finally the whole world realized how unfair it was being, if only the time would come when people treated each other with genuine good will, in the realization that we're all equal and that worldly things are transitory!

How wonderful it is that no one has to wait, but can start right now to gradually change the world! How wonderful it is that everyone, great and small, can immediately help bring about justice by giving of themselves!

As with so many things, most people seek justice in very different quarters, and grumble because they themselves receive so little of it. Open your eyes, be fair in your own dealings first! Give whatever there is to give! You can always—always—give something, even if it's a simple act of kindness! If everyone were to give in this way and didn't scrimp on kindly words, there would be much more love and justice in the world!

Give and you shall receive, much more than you ever thought possible. Give and give again. Keep hoping, keep trying, keep giving! People who give will never be poor!

If you follow this advice, within a few generations, people will never have to feel sorry for poor little beggar children again, because there won't be any!

The world has plenty of room, riches, money and beauty. God has created enough for each and every one of us. Let us begin by dividing it more fairly!

The Wise Old Gnome

Once upon a time there was a little elf named Dora. Dora was rich and beautiful and terribly spoiled by her parents. No one ever saw Dora without a smile on her face. She smiled from early in the morning to late at night. She was happy with everything and never gave a thought to sorrow.

Dora lived in a forest, and in that same forest there was a little gnome named Peldron. Peldron was the exact opposite of Dora: she smiled at the beauty of life, while he wailed at all the misery in the world, especially in the world of elves and gnomes.

One day Dora's mother sent her to the shoemaker's in Elvesville, and what do you think happened? Lo and behold, she ran into the obnoxious and perpetually scowling Peldron. Now, Dora was nice, but since everybody liked her, she was also very stuck-up, and because she was so cocky, she ran over to Peldron, snatched off his adorable gnome's cap and collapsed into giggles a few yards away with the cap in her tiny little hands.

Peldron was furious at the hateful creature; he stamped

his foot and cried, "Give it back, you ugly little imp. Give it back this instant!" But Dora had no intention of giving it back. She ran even farther away, and eventually hid the cap in a hollow log before rushing off to the shoemaker's.

After searching for a long time, Peldron finally found his cap again. He couldn't stand being teased, but most of all he couldn't stand Dora. He was trudging on listlessly when suddenly a deep voice startled him out of his reverie. "Psst, Peldron, over here. I'm the oldest gnome in the world, but also the poorest. Can you spare some change so I can buy some food?"

Peldron shook his head. "I'm not going to give you a thing. You'd be better off dead, because then you wouldn't have to put up with the world's misery any longer," he said, and walked off without so much as a backward glance.

In the meantime, Dora was finished at the shoemaker's, and on the way home the old gnome asked her for some money too. "No," said Dora. "You'll not get a cent from me. You shouldn't have let yourself get into such a fix. The world is too nice a place for me to bother my pretty little head with poor people." And she skipped off.

With a sigh, the old gnome sat down on the moss and thought about how to deal with these two children. One was too sad, the other too happy, and neither of them would get very far in life if they stayed that way.

As it turns out, this gnome, who was so very, very old, was not an ordinary gnome. He was a sorcerer, though by no means an evil one. On the contrary, he wanted to bring out the best in gnomes, elves and people and to make the world a better place. He sat there, thinking, for an hour. Then he got up and walked slowly to the house of Dora's parents.

One day after their encounter in the forest, both Dora and Peldron found themselves locked up in a cottage. They were being held prisoner. The old gnome had taken them from their homes because he wanted to straighten them out, and when he had his heart set on doing good, no parent was allowed to stand in his way.

What were the two of them supposed to do, now that they had been thrown together in the cottage? They weren't allowed to go out, they weren't allowed to argue, they were only allowed to work all day long. These were the three instructions the old gnome had given them. So Dora did her chores, then laughed and joked, and Peldron did his chores, then sat around feeling gloomy. Every evening at seven the old gnome came to see if they had done their work, then left them to fend for themselves.

So what did they have to do to regain their freedom? There was only one way, and that was to do everything the gnome asked them to do. And he was asking a lot. They couldn't go out, they couldn't argue, all they could do was work—those were the gnome's three orders.

Oh, how hard it was for Dora to see no one but the boring Peldron all day long. Everywhere you looked, there was Peldron. Still, Dora barely had time to talk to him, because she had to do the cooking (which her mother had taught her), she had to make sure the house was spic and span and in her spare time, if she had any, she worked at her spinning wheel.

Peldron, on the other hand, chopped wood and dug up the enclosed garden, and when he'd finished his daily chores, he repaired shoes. At seven o'clock Dora called him in to dinner. After that they were both so tired that they could hardly answer the old gnome when he came every evening to check up on their work.

This went on for one whole week. Dora still smiled a lot, but she also began to see the serious side of life, to realize that many people had a hard time of it, so that it was not a bad idea to give them whatever you could rather than send them packing with a flippant remark. Peldron lost some of his gloominess. Why, he even whistled occasionally as he went about his work, or laughed along with Dora at one of her jokes.

On Sunday morning, they were allowed to accompany the old gnome to the busy little chapel in Elvesville. They listened much more carefully to the words of the gnome minister and felt quite contented as they walked back through the green forest.

"And because the two of you have been so good, you may spend the day outside, just as you used to. But remember, you can't visit your family or anyone else, you have to stay together and tomorrow it's back to work!"

Neither of them grumbled, for they were far too happy at being allowed to go into the forest. All day long they danced and looked at the flowers, the birds, the blue sky and especially the warm and friendly sun. And they were content. In the evening, they went back to the cottage as their mentor had instructed them to do. They slept soundly until morning, then trotted off to do their chores.

The old gnome kept them in the cottage for four

whole months. On Sundays they were allowed to go to church and roam around outside, but during the week they worked their fingers to the bone.

One evening, at the end of the four months, the old gnome took them both by the hand and led them into the forest. "Look here, my children. I'm sure you've often been angry at me," he began. "I also think you're longing to go home. Aren't you?"

"Yes," Dora said with a nod. "Yes," said Peldron with another nod.

"But do you understand that being here has done you good?"

No, neither Dora nor Peldron understood what he meant. "Well, then, I'll explain it to you," the old gnome said. "I brought you here so that you would learn that there is more to life than your own pleasure and sorrow. You'll now be able to deal with life much better than you did before. Dora has become a bit more serious and Peldron a bit more cheerful, precisely because you were forced to make the best of the situation in which you found yourselves. I believe you two get along with each other much better now. Wouldn't you say so, Peldron?"

"Oh, yes, I think Dora's a lot nicer than I used to," the little gnome answered.

"In that case, you may go home to your parents. Think back sometimes to your stay in this wooden cottage. Enjoy the good things that life has to offer, but don't forget the sad things, and do what you can to help lessen the sorrow. All people can help each other; all gnomes and elves too. Even little elves like Dora and little gnomes like Peldron can do quite a lot. So, go on your way and don't be angry with me anymore. I did what I could for you, and all for your own good. Farewell, my children, till we meet again."

"Bye-bye," said Dora and Peldron, and off they went to their separate homes.

The old gnome sat down in the grass. He had just one wish, and that was to get all children on the right path as quickly as he had these two.

Indeed, Dora and Peldron lived happily ever after. They had learned once and for all that there are appropriate moments for both laughter and tears. Later, much later, when they had grown up, they even decided to share a house, and Dora did the chores inside and Peldron the chores outside, just as they had when they were children!

Blurry the Explorer

Sunday, April 23, 1944

Once, when Blurry was a very little bear, he felt a terrible urge to get away from his mother's care for a while and see a bit of the big wide world for himself.

For days, he was so busy trying to come up with a plan that he wasn't his usual lively self. But on the evening of the fourth day, it "hit" him. Now that his plan was ready, all he had to do was carry it out. Early the next morning he would go into the garden, quietly of course so that Miesje, his little mistress, wouldn't notice, then he'd crawl through a hole in the hedge and after that . . . well, after that he'd go out and discover the world!

All of which he did, and so quietly that he had already been gone for several hours before anyone noticed that he'd made his escape.

His fur was completely covered with dirt and mud when he emerged from the hedge, but a bear, especially a little teddy bear out to discover the world, couldn't be bothered by a little thing like dirt! So, with his eyes on the ground to keep from stumbling over the bumpy cobblestones, Blurry stepped jauntily down the alleyway between the gardens and into the street.

Once there, he was startled for a moment by the many tall people, whose long legs seemed to swallow him up. "I'd better move over to the side to keep from getting trampled," he thought, and that was in fact the most sensible thing to do. Blurry was a sensible bear, no doubt about it, for, despite his tender age, he wanted to discover the world all by himself!

So he kept to the side and made sure he didn't get crushed. But suddenly his heart began pounding like a sledgehammer. What on earth was that? A huge, dark, black abyss was yawning at his feet. The trapdoor to a cellar had been left open, but Blurry didn't know that, and his head began to spin. Would he have to go in there?

He cast an anxious glance in all directions, but the stockinged legs of the ladies and the trousered legs of the gentlemen were going around the dark hole as if nothing were the matter. Not quite recovered from his fright, Blurry inched his way past it, step by step, until he was able to continue along the wall normally again.

"Well, I'm out in the big wide world now, but where is it? I can't see the world through all these stockings and trousers," Blurry thought to himself. "I guess I'm too small to go exploring. But I don't care. The older I get, the taller I'll be, and if I drink my milk with the skin on it (the very thought of it made him shudder), I'll be as tall as all of these people. So I guess I should just keep on going, and sooner or later I'm bound to bump into the world."

*   *   *

Blurry therefore walked on, taking as little notice as he could of the many legs, both fat and thin, around him. But . . . did he have to keep walking? He was very hungry, and it was also starting to get dark. Blurry hadn't thought of that—that he'd have to eat and sleep. He'd been so full of exploration plans that he'd forgotten all about such ordinary and unheroic things as eating and sleeping.

Sighing, he kept walking for a while, until he discovered an open door. For a moment he hesitated. Then he made up his mind and tiptoed inside. He was in luck, because, after going through another door, he saw two food bowls on the floor between four wooden legs. There was milk with skin on it in one of the bowls, and hash of some kind in the other. Starving, and eager to try such delicious food, Blurry first gulped down the milk, skin and all—as grown-up bears should—then immediately polished off the hash. He was happy and full.

But, oh, horrors, what was that? A white creature with huge green eyes was slowly creeping forward and staring straight at him. It stopped directly in front of him and asked in a high-pitched voice, "Who are you and why have you eaten my food?"

"I'm Blurry, and I need to eat if I'm going to see the big wide world, which is why I ate your dinner, though I didn't know it was yours!"

"Ah, so you're out exploring the world. But why did you have to explore my food bowl?"

"Because I didn't see any others," Blurry said, in as unfriendly a voice as he could muster. Then he thought better of it and asked in a friendlier tone, "So, what's your name and what kind of strange creature are you?"

"I'm Mirwa and I'm an Angora cat. I'm extremely

valuable. Anyway, that's what my mistress always says. But you know, Blurry, I'm lonely and bored a lot of the time. Will you stay here and keep me company for a while?"

"I'm willing to spend the night," Blurry replied firmly, with an air of doing the beautiful Mirwa a favor. "But tomorrow I have to get back to exploring!"

Mirwa was happy to leave it at that for the time being. "Come with me," she said, and Blurry followed her into another room, which was filled with legs—wooden legs, both big ones and small ones—but also . . . over in the corner, a large wicker basket with a green silk cushion. Mirwa leapt right onto that cushion with her dirty feet, but Blurry thought it would be a shame to get it dirty.

"Can't you clean me up a bit first?" he asked.

"Of course," she said. "I'll wash you the same way I wash myself."

Blurry wasn't at all familiar with her method, which was just as well, since if he'd known he would never have let her begin. Anyway, the cat ordered him to stand up, then proceeded very calmly to lick his feet with her tongue. Blurry shivered and anxiously asked Mirwa whether that was the way she usually washed herself.

"Of course," she said. "Wait and see how clean you'll be. You'll be all shiny and sleek, and since shiny teddy bears are welcome everywhere, you'll get to see even more of the world!"

Blurry tried to hide his shivers. And like a brave little teddy bear, he didn't utter another peep.

The cat's washing took a very long time. Blurry was starting to get impatient and his feet hurt from having to stand so long. But finally . . . finally, his fur was shiny again!

Mirwa climbed back into the basket and Blurry, who was exhausted, lay down beside her. Mirwa tucked him in, you might say, by covering him with her furry coat, since she was practically lying on top of him. Within five minutes, they were both fast asleep.

The next morning Blurry woke up bewildered, and it was several moments before he figured out what was on top of him. Mirwa was snoring a little, and Blurry was dying to have breakfast. So, without a thought to the comfort of his gracious hostess, he shook her off and immediately began issuing orders: "My breakfast now, please, Mirwa. I'm starving!"

Mirwa had a good yawn, stretched herself out until she was twice as long as usual, then replied, "No, you've had all you're going to get. My mistress mustn't notice you're here. You'll have to sneak out through the garden as quick as you can!" And Mirwa sprang out of her basket, raced across the room, out one door, in another, out again—through a glass door this time—and they found themselves outside. "Goodbye, Blurry, have a good trip." And she was gone.

Lonely and not at all sure of himself anymore (a change that must have come over him in the night), Blurry scampered across the garden, under the hedge and into the street. Where was he supposed to go now, and how long would it be before he discovered the world? Blurry had no idea.

He was slowly making his way down the street when a

huge four-legged beast suddenly came charging around the corner at full speed. It was making such a frightful noise that Blurry's ears hurt. Terrified, he pressed himself as tightly as he could against the side of a house. The monster stopped a few feet away, then started coming closer. Blurry was so scared he began to cry, but the huge whatever-it-was didn't seem to care. On the contrary, it sat down and kept staring, wide-eyed, at the poor little teddy bear.

Blurry was shaking from head to toe, but all of a sudden he plucked up his courage enough to ask, "What do you want?"

"I just want to look at you, because I've never seen anything like you before."

Blurry breathed a sigh of relief. Apparently you could talk to the creature. That was odd, because why didn't his own mistress ever understand what he said? Still, he didn't have time to ponder this weighty question, because just then the huge animal opened its mouth so wide you could see every one of its teeth. Blurry shivered, much more than he had when Mirwa was licking him clean. What was that frightful creature going to do with him?

The answer came sooner than he would have liked, for, without so much as a by-your-leave, the animal grabbed him by the neck and started dragging him down the street. Blurry couldn't cry anymore, since he'd choke to death if he did, and screaming was totally out of the question, so all he could do was tremble, which did nothing to boost his courage.

At least he didn't have to walk. If his neck wasn't hurting so much, it wouldn't be so bad, kind of like going for a ride. Actually, it wasn't that awful. Hmm, all those thumpity-thumps made you sleepy. Where's my ride taking me? Where's my . . . Where's . . . ? Blurry, clutched firmly in the creature's mouth, had dozed off.

But his nap didn't last long, because the big beast suddenly wondered what he was doing with this thing between his teeth. So he blithely let go of Blurry, after first chomping down hard on his neck, and then ran off.

The helpless little teddy bear who had wanted to see the world lay there on the ground, all alone and in pain. Still, he managed to scramble to his feet so he wouldn't get stepped on. Rubbing his eyes, he looked around. Far fewer legs, far fewer walls, much more sun and not as many cobblestones beneath your feet. Was this the world?

His head was throbbing and pounding so badly that he couldn't think. He didn't want to walk anymore. Why should he? Where would he go? Mirwa was far away, his mother was even farther, and with her little mistress. No, now that he'd left, he had to keep going until he'd discovered the world.

Startled by a noise behind him, he quickly turned his head. Not another beast that was going to bite him? No, this time it was a little girl who had found Blurry.

"Look, Mommy, a teddy bear. Can I take it home with me?" she asked her mother, who had followed behind her.

"No, it's filthy. Besides, it's bleeding!"

"That doesn't matter, we can wash it off when we get home. I'm going to take it with me so I'll have something to play with."

Blurry couldn't understand a word, since his little ears were only used to animal talk. But the little girl with the blond hair seemed nice, so he didn't put up a struggle when she wrapped him in a cloth and tucked him in her bag. Rocking back and forth, Blurry continued on his travels through the world.

After the little girl had walked for a while, she took Blurry, still wrapped in the cloth, out of her bag and propped him up on her arm. That was a lucky break—he could now look at the street from above for the first time.

What a lot of bricks there were, and look how high they'd been stacked, with here and there an opening. And that thing on top, up near the sky—it must be some kind of decoration, like the feather on his mistress's hat. There was a plume of smoke coming out of it. Do you suppose it had a cigarette in its mouth, one of those thin ones that the master of the house was always smoking? Such a funny sight! But above the bricks there was apparently even more space, because there was a bit of blue. Oh, look, it was moving. Something white came and covered up the blue, drifting closer and closer until it was right above their heads, and then it kept on drifting until once more the area above that tall smoking thing was as blue as it had been before.

Down on the street, something honked and whizzed by. But where were its legs and feet? It didn't have any. Instead, there were a couple of round inflated things. Oh my, going out to see the world was certainly worth the effort. What could you learn by sitting at home? Why else had you been born? Not to stay at your mother's side forever and ever, but to see things, do things. That's why he wanted to grow up. Oh, yes, Blurry knew what he wanted.

Finally . . . finally, the little girl came to a halt beside a door. She went in, and the first thing Blurry saw was the same kind of creature as Mirwa, a "cat," it was called, if he remembered correctly. This cat rubbed itself against the little blond girl's legs, but she pushed him aside and, still carrying Blurry, walked over to one of those white things that his mistress had at home too, though Blurry had forgotten its name. It was high up off the floor—broad, white and smooth. On one side there was a shiny metal object that could be turned, and that's just what the little blond girl did. She set Blurry down on top of the hard cold surface and began to wash him, especially his neck, where he'd been bitten by that awful beast. It hurt, and Blurry growled a lot, but no one paid the slightest bit of attention.

Fortunately, this washing didn't last as long as Mirwa's had . . . though it was a lot colder and wetter. The little girl was through fairly quickly. She dried him off, wrapped him in a clean cloth and tucked him into a moving bed, just like the one his little mistress was always putting him in.

Why did he have to go to bed now? Blurry wasn't the least bit tired and didn't want to go to bed. As soon as the little girl left the room, Blurry slipped out of bed and wandered through a large number of doors and openings until he once again found himself on the street.

"It's definitely time for me to eat," Blurry thought. He sniffed. There must be food nearby, since he could smell it. Following his nose, he soon came to the door from which the appetizing smell was coming. He slipped past a pair of stockinged legs and into the shop.

Two young girls, standing behind a big, tall object of some kind, caught sight of Blurry almost immediately. They had to work long hard hours and could use a little extra help. So they snatched him up and put him in a dimly lit room, which was incredibly hot.

It wasn't so bad, however, since you could eat as much as you wanted. The floor, the benches—everywhere you looked there were rows and rows of cakes and buns. Blurry had never seen so many of them, or such pretty ones. Just what had Blurry ever seen? Not much, in fact! He dug in, eating so many pastries that he almost made himself sick.

When he was done, he took a better look around, for there was indeed a lot to see. It was the land of plenty: breads, buns, cakes and cookies galore, all for the taking, and it was very busy—Blurry saw lots of white legs, not at all like the ones he'd seen on the street.

He didn't have much time for daydreaming. The girls, who had been watching him from a distance, now shoved a big broom into his hands and showed him how to use it. Humph, sweeping floors was going to be a snap. Blurry's mother used to sweep sometimes; he'd seen her do it often enough.

He gamely got to work, but it wasn't as easy as it looked. The broom was heavy and the dust tickled his nose so badly that it made him sneeze. Besides, it was hot and he wasn't used to doing this kind of work in the heat, so that he felt like he was suffocating, but every time he stopped to rest for a moment someone would order him back to work and box his ears to boot.

"If only I hadn't rushed in here," he thought to himself, "I would have been spared all this ghastly work." But it was no use now. He had no choice but to sweep, so he swept.

After he had been sweeping for a long time—long enough for the dirt to be piled into a big heap—one of the girls took him by the hand and led him to a corner, where there was a pile of hard, yellowish, curly things. She laid him down on top of these, and Blurry understood that he could now go to sleep.

Comfortable, as if it were the finest of beds, Blurry stretched himself out and slept, and he went on sleeping until the next morning.

At seven o'clock he had to get up. Again he was allowed to eat as many pastries as he wanted, and again he was put to work. Poor Blurry, he wasn't even rested from the long and exhausting hours he'd put in the day before. He wasn't used to working and the heat bothered him no end. His head, arms and legs ached, and he felt as though his entire body was swollen.

And now, for the first time, he began to long for home, for his mother, for his little mistress, for his comfy bed and his easy life . . . but how was he to get there? He'd never be able to escape. The two girls watched his every move, and besides, the one and only door led to the room they were in. Even if he could get that far, they would be sure to stop him. No, Blurry would just have to wait!

His thoughts were all in a jumble, and he felt sick and

weak. The room began to spin, so he sat down. Nobody scolded him. When the dizzy spell was over, he got back to work.

One can get used to anything. And so it was with Blurry. After a week of sweeping from early in the morning to late at night, he felt as if he'd been doing it forever.

Little bears forget quickly, which is just as well. Still, Blurry had not forgotten his mother or his home. It's just that they seemed so unreal and so far away!

Then one night the two girls who were holding the little bear hostage saw the following notice in the newspaper:

REWARD PROMISED FOR THE SAFE RETURN OF A LITTLE BROWN BEAR ANSWERING TO THE NAME OF BLURRY.

"Do you think it might be our bear?" they asked each other. "He doesn't work very hard anyway. You can't expect such a small animal to do very much, so if we get a reward for bringing him back we'll probably be better off." They quickly walked to the back, where the bakery was, and shouted, "Blurry!"

Blurry looked up from his work. Was somebody calling his name? He let go of the broom and perked up his ears even more.

The girls came closer and shouted again, "Blurry!" Blurry raced over to where they were.

"He's called Blurry, all right. That's as plain as day," one of the girls said to the other. "Let's take him back tonight." And so it was agreed. That very same evening, Blurry was delivered to the house of his little mistress, and the two girls collected their reward.

From his mistress, Blurry got a spanking for being so naughty and then a kiss for being back home again. From his mother, he got nothing but the following questions:

"Why did you run away, Blurry?"

"Because I wanted to discover the world," he said.

"And did you?"

"Oh, I saw lots and lots of things. I'm now a much more experienced bear!"

"Yes, I know that. But I asked if you'd discovered the world?"

"Uh . . . no . . . not exactly. I couldn't find it!"

The Fairy

❧

Friday, May 12, 1944

The fairy I'm talking about was no ordinary fairy, like the ones you usually see in fairyland. Oh, no, my fairy was quite an exceptional fairy—exceptional in looks and exceptional in behavior. Just what was it, you're no doubt asking yourself, that made this fairy so exceptional?

Well, not because she did a little good here and had a little fun there, but because she had taken it upon herself to bring joy to people and the world.

The name of this exceptional fairy was Ellen. Her parents died when she was very young, but they left her quite a bit of money. So, when Ellen was a little girl, she could do as she wished and buy whatever she wanted. Other children or elves or fairies might have been spoiled rotten by this, but since Ellen had always been so exceptional, she wasn't in the least bit spoiled. As she grew older, she still had quite a lot of money, but all she ever did with it was buy beautiful clothes and eat delicious food.

One morning Ellen woke up, and as she lay in her soft little bed, she thought about what to do with her money.

"I can't spend it all on myself and I can't take it with me to the grave. So why don't I use it to make other people happy?" That was a good plan, and Ellen was anxious to get started right away. So she got up, put on her clothes, grabbed a wicker basket, filled it with money from one of her many bundles and left the house.

"Where shall I begin?" she wondered. "Wait, I know. The woodcutter's widow will be pleased to have a visit from me. Her husband just died, and the poor woman must be having a difficult time."

Singing, Ellen made her way through the grass and knocked at the door of the woodcutter's little cottage. "Come in," called a voice from inside. She gently opened the door and stuck her head around it. On the far side of the dark room, a little old lady was sitting in a rickety armchair, knitting.

She was very surprised when Ellen came in and laid a handful of money on the table. Like everyone else, the old woman knew that you must never refuse the gifts of fairies and elves, so she graciously said, "That's very kind of you, my child. Not very many people would give something for nothing, but luckily the inhabitants of fairyland are different."

Ellen looked at her in amazement. "What do you mean by that?" she asked.

"Well, I mean that very few people give something away without expecting something else in return."

"Oh, no? But why would I want anything from you? I'm truly glad that my basket is a little lighter now."

"Then all is well. Thank you very much."

Ellen said goodbye and continued on her way. After walking for ten minutes, she found herself at the next cottage. She knocked, even though she didn't know the people who lived there. As soon as she had opened the door, Ellen could see that they weren't in need of money. The people in this house weren't lacking in material goods, but in happiness.

The woman received her kindly enough, though she wasn't very cheerful. Her eyes didn't sparkle, and she looked sad.

Ellen decided to stay a little longer. "Perhaps I can help this woman in some other way," she thought, and sure enough, the moment the nice little fairy had seated herself on a cushion, the woman began, with no prompting, to pour out her woes. She talked about her worthless husband, her naughty children and her many disappointments. Ellen listened, asked an occasional question and got very involved in the woman's suffering. When the woman finally reached the end of her tale, the two of them sat for a few moments in silence.

Then Ellen began to speak. "You poor dear," she said. "I've never suffered like you have, nor do I have any experience with this kind of thing, much less know how to help you, yet I'd like to offer you some advice—something that I myself find useful when I'm feeling as lonely and as sad as you do. One morning, when it's quiet and beautiful, take a walk through the woods, you know the one I mean, the one going to the heath. After you've walked through the heather for a while, sit down somewhere and do nothing. Just look at the sky and the trees. You'll feel a calm come over you, and suddenly none of your problems will seem so bad that they can't be fixed."

"Oh, no, fairy. I doubt if that remedy of yours is going to help me any more than all the other potions I've tried."

"Just give it a chance," Ellen urged her. "When you're alone with nature, your troubles will seem to melt away, I'm sure they will. You'll become thoughtful and glad and feel as if God hasn't forsaken you after all."

"If it will make you happy, I'll try," the woman replied.

"Good. Well, I'd better be going. I'll stop by at the same time next week."

And so Ellen went into nearly every house, cheering up the people inside, and at the end of the long day her basket was empty and her heart was full, because she felt as if her money and talents had been truly well spent, much better than on expensive clothes.

After that day Ellen often set forth with her basket on her arm, dressed in her flowery yellow dress with a big bow in her hair. And she went into people's homes and made all of them happy.

The woman who had enough money and more than enough sorrow had also become much more cheerful, as Ellen knew she would. Her remedy always worked!

As a result of all her visits, Ellen had many friends. Not just fairies and elves, but ordinary men, women and children, who told her about their lives. So Ellen got lots of experience, and before long she had a suitable answer for every problem.

But as for her money . . . Well, her calculations were a bit off, because after a year the lion's share was gone. She now had just enough to live on.

If you think that made Ellen sad or kept her from giving to others, you're wrong. Ellen continued to give—not money, but good advice and loving words.

Yes, indeed, Ellen had learned that even when you're

the only one left of a large family, you can still make your life beautiful, and that no matter how poor you are, you can still help others enjoy their inner riches.

Ellen died when she was a very old fairy, and never before in the entire world had so many tears been shed. Yet Ellen's spirit was still alive, for she often came back when people were asleep and made sure they had pleasant dreams, so that in their sleep they could still benefit from the advice of the extraordinary Ellen.

Riek

❧

It was quarter past four, and I was walking down a fairly quiet street and had just decided to go into the nearest bakery when two teenage girls, walking arm in arm and talking a mile a minute, came out of a side street and started going in my direction.

People everywhere find it interesting and refreshing to hear two teenage girls talking from time to time, not just because they laugh and giggle at the slightest thing, but also because their laughter is so infectious that everyone around them can't help laughing too.

And so it went with me. As I walked behind the two girls, I listened to their conversation, which in this case revolved around the ten cents they had to spend on sweets. They debated excitedly about what they could buy for that amount of money, their mouths already watering at each tantalizing suggestion. When they reached the bakery, the two girls continued to discuss their choices outside the display window, and because I was behind them looking at the goodies too, I knew what they'd decided on even before they entered the shop.

It wasn't busy, so the two girls were soon being waited on. They had chosen two good-sized tarts, which—miracle of miracles—they managed to take out of the shop uneaten. Then it was my turn, and half a minute later I saw the pair of them just up the street, talking loudly once again.

On the next corner was another bakery. A little girl was standing in front of the window, staring hungrily at the pastries. The two lucky owners of the tarts stopped beside the poor child to look at this display as well and quickly struck up a conversation with her. By the time I reached the corner, they had already been talking for a while, so I heard only the last part of the conversation.

"Oh my, are you that hungry?" one of the girls asked the child. "Would you like to have my tart?" The child nodded.

"Don't be ridiculous, Riek," the other girl exclaimed. "Eat it right away, like I did. If you give it to her, you won't even get a taste!"

Riek didn't answer, but looked hesitantly back and forth between the tart and the little girl. Then she suddenly handed the child the tart, saying kindly, "Please take it. I have tonight's dinner to look forward to!" And before the little girl by the window could even say thank you, the two teenagers had disappeared from view.

I also continued on my way, and as I went past the little girl, who was savoring her tart, she said to me, "Would you like a bite, miss? Somebody just gave it to me."

I thanked her and walked on with a smile. Who do you think enjoyed it most: Riek, her girlfriend or the little girl?

I think Riek did!

Jo

❦

Undated

Jo stands beside the open window in her bedroom and takes a deep breath of fresh air. She's hot, and the air feels good on her tear-stained face.

She raises her eyes higher and higher until they finally come to rest on the moon and the stars.

"Oh," she moans. "I can't go on, I can't even summon the energy to feel sad. Paul has left me, I'm all alone, perhaps for good, but I just can't go on, I can't do anything, I only know how desperate I feel." And while Jo keeps on gazing at nature, which is revealing itself in all its splendor tonight, she grows calm. While the wind whips through the trees outside the house, while the sky darkens and the stars take cover behind the big, thick clouds, looking like so many wads of blotting paper in the cloudy light and forming every imaginable shape, Jo suddenly feels that she's not at all desperate, that she is indeed capable of doing something, that no one can take away her inner happiness, which is hers and hers alone. "No one," she whispers, without being aware of it. "Not even Paul."

After standing at the window for an hour, Jo has recovered. She's still sad, but no longer desperate. Everyone who takes a long and deep enough look into nature—and therefore into themselves—will be cured, just as Jo was, of all despair.

Why?

❧

Undated

Ever since I was a little girl and could barely talk, the word "why" has lived and grown along with me. It's a well-known fact that children ask questions about anything and everything, since almost everything is new to them. That was especially true of me, and not just as a child. Even when I was older, I couldn't stop asking questions. That wasn't necessarily bad, and I must admit that my parents patiently answered my questions until . . . until I started pestering strangers too. Not all people can stand being bombarded with children's questions.

I have to admit that it can be annoying sometimes, but I comfort myself with the thought that "You won't know until you ask," though by now I've asked so much that they ought to have made me a professor.

When I got older, I noticed that not all questions can be asked and that many whys can never be answered. As a result, I tried to work things out for myself by mulling over my own questions. And I came to the important discovery that questions which you either can't or shouldn't ask in public, or questions which you can't put into words, can easily be solved in your own head. So the word "why" not only taught me to ask, but also to think.

And now for the second aspect of the word "why." I believe that if everyone asked themselves "why?" before they did something, they'd be much better persons, and also much more honest. The best way to become good and honest is never to pass up an opportunity for self-examination.

The most cowardly thing a person can do is not admit to himself his own faults and shortcomings, which we all have. This applies to both children and adults, since in this respect they're alike. Most people think that parents are supposed to raise their children and try to develop their characters to the best of their ability, but that's not true.

From an early age, children need to raise themselves and develop their own characters. A lot of people might think this sounds crazy, but it's not. A child, no matter how young, is a person with a conscience of his own. Getting a child to realize that his own conscience punishes him far more severely is a large part of child-rearing.

To fourteen- and fifteen-year-olds, any form of punishment is ridiculous, since at that age they know that no one, not even their own parents, can accomplish anything by punishing them, physically or otherwise. By reasoning with them and confronting them with their own behavior you will achieve results faster than with the most severe of punishments.

But I didn't intend this to be a lecture on child-rearing. All I wanted to say was that in the lives of every child and adult, the word "why" plays a significant role, as indeed it should.

The saying "You won't know until you ask" is true to the extent that it gets people to think. And thinking has never hurt anyone. On the contrary, it does us all a world of good.

Who Is Interesting?

Undated

A week ago I was sitting in a train, chugging along to my aunt's in Bussum. I was hoping to be able to amuse myself in the train at least, since having to put up with a week of Aunt Josephine's company was not my idea of fun.

So there I sat, with the highest of hopes, but I was out of luck, because at first sight my fellow passengers looked neither interesting nor amusing. The little old lady across from me was indeed concerned for my welfare, but wasn't the least bit amusing; neither was the distinguished gentleman beside her, who kept his eyes glued to his newspaper; nor did the farm woman on the other side of him look like she was dying to talk. Still, I was determined to amuse myself, and wasn't about to give up my plan. If I had to make a pest of myself, so be it. Aunt Josephine and her scrawny neck would just have to take the blame.

After fifteen minutes with nothing to show for it, I didn't look a bit more amusing than the other passengers in my compartment. However, the train made its first stop and, to my great delight, a man of about thirty got in. He didn't look amusing, but he did look interesting.

The general consensus among women is that men with youthful faces and graying temples are interesting, and I had never doubted the truth of this. Now I could put one of these gentlemen to the test, or at any rate not let his interesting looks go to waste.

The big question now was: How was I to get Mr. Interesting to show me how interesting he was? Another fifteen minutes must have gone by before I suddenly hit upon the simple but time-honored trick of dropping my handkerchief. The results were spectacular. Not only because the interesting gentleman very gallantly (what else could you expect?) scooped up my handkerchief from the filthy floor, but also because he took advantage of the opportunity to strike up a conversation with me.

"Excuse me, miss," he began quite openly, though of course he kept his voice down, since there was no need for the other passengers to hear us. "I believe this belongs to you. But in exchange for your handkerchief, I'd like to know your name!"

To be honest, I thought he was rather bold, but since I was determined to have a good time, I replied in a similar vein, "Well, of course, sir. It's Miss van Bergen."

He gave me a reproachful look, then suavely said, "Oh, but I'd like to know your first name!"

"Well, okay, it's Hetty," I replied.

"Ah, Hetty," he repeated, and we chatted for a while about this and that. But for the life of me I couldn't turn it into an interesting conversation. That, I felt, was up to the gentleman, who, in the eyes of the world, was supposed to be interesting.

He got out at the next station, and I was greatly disappointed. However, the little old lady across from me suddenly unwound and started talking to me. She was so funny and interesting that the time simply flew by, and before I knew it, I'd reached my destination. I thanked the interesting old lady, and I now know that so-called interesting men owe their reputation to their looks alone.

So, if you're hoping to amuse yourself during a trip or whatever, do as I do and look around for people who are old or ugly. They're sure to entertain you more than the men whose faces are all but glowing with conceit.

Cady's Life

I have lots of ideas and am busy trying to put the bits and pieces together. To give me an overall view and because I haven't got any more lined paper, I'm writing everything down at the back of this diary. *

Chapter 1

When Cady opened her eyes, the first thing she noticed was that everything around her was white. Her last clear memory was of someone shouting at her . . . a car . . . falling down . . . then everything went black. She now felt a stab of pain in her right leg and left arm, and though she didn't realize it, she was moaning softly. A friendly face, looking out from under a white cap, promptly bent over her.

"You poor thing, does it hurt a lot? Do you remember what happened to you?" the nurse asked.

"Oh, it's nothing . . ."

The nurse smiled. Cady continued, though she had to make an effort to talk, "Yes . . . a car . . . I fell . . . then I don't know!"

"If you could just tell me your name, we'll contact your parents so they can come see you and stop wondering what happened to you."

---

*Written at the back of Diary 2, the second volume of Anne's diary.

Cady was visibly shaken. "But . . . but . . . uh . . ." was all she managed to say.

"Don't worry. Your parents haven't been waiting all that long. You've only been here for about an hour."

Cady managed a weak smile, though it wasn't easy. "My name is Caroline Dorothea van Altenhoven, or Cady for short, and I live at 261 Zuider Amstellaan."

"Are you anxious to see your parents?"

Cady merely nodded. She was so tired and everything hurt so much; one more sigh, and she had fallen asleep.

Nurse Ank, keeping watch beside the bed in the little white room, looked worriedly at the small, pale face lying so quietly on the pillow as if nothing were wrong. But something was very wrong. According to what she had heard from the doctor, the girl had been hit by a car that had come around the corner just as she was about to cross the street. She fell, but luckily the car had good brakes, so it didn't run completely over her. According to the doctor, she had a compound fracture of the right leg, her left arm was badly hurt and her left foot had also been injured. Would this sweet child ever be able to walk again? Nurse Ank was very doubtful; the doctor had looked extremely grave. Fortunately, the child herself suspected nothing, and would be told as little of the truth as possible. Cady moaned in her sleep, startling Nurse Ank out of her reverie. Since there was nothing she could do to help the girl, she quickly stood up, pressed a button and handed the nurse who came in a piece of paper with the name and address of the van Altenhovens.

"Try to find their number in the phone book, then gently inform them of their daughter's condition. Ask them to come to the hospital as soon as possible. If you can't find their phone number, send a boy around with a note!"

The door closed again without a sound. Sighing, Nurse Ank picked up her knitting from the bedside table. She was thinking such gloomy thoughts this afternoon. Why did this girl's future affect her so much? Hadn't she seen many people who had been crippled for life in accidents just like this one? Hadn't she learned to switch off her feelings long ago? But it didn't help. Her thoughts kept coming back to the same subject.

There was a gentle knock at the door. A nurse ushered in a woman of medium height, and an unusually tall and handsome man. Nurse Ank stood up—they had to be Cady's parents. Mrs. van Altenhoven was quite pale and looked at her daughter with fear in her eyes, but Cady was still sleeping peacefully and didn't notice.

"Oh, Nurse, tell me what happened. We waited and waited for her, but we never imagined there'd been an accident . . . no . . . no . . ."

"You mustn't worry too much, Mrs. van Altenhoven Your daughter has already regained consciousness." Nurse Ank then told them what she knew of the case, and in trying not to make it sound too hopeless, she felt herself becoming more hopeful and happy again. Who knows, perhaps the child really would get better!

While the grown-ups were talking, Cady woke up, and when she saw that her parents were there, she suddenly felt a lot worse than when she and the nurse had been alone together. Now all kinds of thoughts came crowding into her head, horrible images that attacked her from all sides. She saw herself crippled for life . . . with only one arm . . . and other images too awful to think about.

Meanwhile, Mrs. van Altenhoven had noticed that Cady was awake, and she went over to the bed. "Does it hurt? How are you feeling now? Would you like me to stay? Can I get you anything?"

There was no way Cady could answer all these questions. So she simply nodded and longed for the moment when all the fuss would be over.

"Father!" was all she managed to say.

Mr. van Altenhoven sat down on the edge of the big iron bed and, without saying a word or asking a question, took his daughter's one good hand in his.

"Oh, thank you, thank you . . ." And Cady said no more, for she had fallen asleep again.

Chapter 2

A week had gone by since the accident. Cady's mother came every morning and afternoon, but she wasn't allowed to stay long since her constant nervous chatter wore Cady out, and the nurse who took care of her had noticed that Cady looked forward to her father's visits much more than to her mother's.

The nurse had almost no trouble at all with her little patient. Though Cady must have been in a great deal of pain, especially when she was being examined by the doctor, she never complained and was never unhappy.

She preferred to lie quietly and daydream while Nurse Ank sat beside the bed, knitting or reading. After the first few days, Cady no longer slept all the time. She liked to talk every now and then, and there was no one she liked to talk to better than Nurse Ank, who was always so calm and talked in such a gentle voice. Her gentleness was what appealed to Cady the most. Only now did Cady realize that she had never before received such motherly love and tenderness. Little by little, a sense of trust began to develop between the two, and the nurse began asking Cady questions about all kinds of things.

One morning, at the end of the first two weeks, when Cady had already confided so much to her, Nurse Ank cautiously asked about her mother. Cady had been expecting the question and it came as a relief to share her feelings for a change.

"Why do you ask? Do you think I was unkind to Mother?"

"No, that's not what I meant. It's just that I get the feeling you treat your mother differently than you do your father, a bit cooler perhaps."

"That's true. I can't seem to feel any real affection for my mother, and it breaks my heart. Mother and I are very different. That wouldn't be so bad, except that she shows so little understanding of the things I think are important and that mean a lot to me. Can you help me, Nurse Ank? Can you tell me how to change my attitude toward my mother so she won't feel that I don't love her as much as I do my father? Because I know that Mother loves me, her only child, very much!"

"She means well. I think she just doesn't know how to approach you. Perhaps she's basically shy and insecure?"

"Oh, no. That's not it. She thinks she's the perfect mother. She'd be astonished if someone told her she didn't know how to approach me. She clearly thinks I'm the one to blame. Nurse Ank, you're just the mother I'd like to have. I long so much for a real mother, yet the woman who is my mother will never be able to fulfill that role.

"There isn't a soul on earth who's completely happy with what they've got, though most people would say I have everything I need. I have a comfortable home, my parents get along well and I get whatever my little heart desires, but doesn't a real, understanding mother play a big part in a girl's life? Or maybe not just a girl's life? How do I know what boys think and feel? I've never really gotten close to a boy. But they must have the same need for an understanding mother, though perhaps they express it differently!

"It just occurred to me that what Mother lacks is tact. She talks so unfeelingly about the most sensitive subjects. She understands nothing of what's going on inside me, and yet she's always saying she's so interested in adolescents. She doesn't know the first thing about patience and gentleness. She may be a woman, but she's not a real mother!"

"Don't be too hard on your mother, Cady. Perhaps she's different because she's been through a lot and now prefers to avoid anything that might be painful."

"I don't know. What does a daughter like me know about the lives of her parents? Or about her mother's life? Do they ever tell her anything? It's precisely because I don't understand Mother and she doesn't understand me that we've never trusted and confided in each other."

"And your father, Cady?"

"Father knows that Mother and I have different personalities. He understands both Mother and me. He's a sweetheart, Nurse Ank, and he tries to make up for what I don't get from Mother. It's just that he's afraid to talk about the subject and avoids any conversations that might lead to it. A man can do a lot, but he can never take the place of a mother!"

"I wish I could tell you otherwise, Cady, but I can't, because I know you're right. It's a shame you and your mother find yourselves in opposite corners instead of on the same side. Do you think things will ever get better, especially when you're older?"

Cady shrugged almost imperceptibly. "I miss having a mother so badly. It would mean so much to me to have someone I could trust and confide in completely and who would do the same with me!"

"Cady, I'm very fond of you and I wish I could give you what you're asking for, but I don't believe I could ever be what you expect me to be. I could tell you many things, also about myself, but there can never be the kind of trust between us that exists between a mother and a daughter or between two girlfriends, because that kind of trust has to grow!"

At Nurse Ank's words, Cady's eyes filled with tears. When she came to the end, Cady held out her hand, since she wasn't able to sit up yet, but Nurse Ank understood what it was she wanted to say.

"Oh, Nurse Ank, it's a terrible blow for me, but you're right. I can give you my trust, but you can't give me yours."

Cady fell silent and Nurse Ank looked very grave. "Let's not talk about it anymore just now, my dear. Still, it's good that you told me what you did about your mother." And, abruptly changing the subject, she added, "I almost forgot, I've got news for you. If you keep making such good progress, your friends will be allowed to come visit you, one at a time, starting next week!"

You could see from Cady's eyes that she was elated at the news. Not so much because she'd be able to see her friends again, but because it was the clearest proof she'd had so far that she was getting better.

Happy and relieved, she ate the bowl of oatmeal that was brought to her bed, then lay down for her afternoon nap.

Chapter 3

And so the weeks went by rather monotonously for Cady. Many of her friends and acquaintances came to visit, but she was still alone for most of the day. Her condition had now improved so much that she was allowed to sit up and read. She had been given a lap desk, and her father had bought her a diary, so she now often sat up and jotted down her thoughts and feelings. Cady had never realized how pleasant and diverting this could be.

Nurse Ank, who now had other patients to attend to, kept up her practice of sitting and talking to Cady for half an hour every morning, after she had washed her and gotten her ready for breakfast.

Life in the hospital was monotonous indeed, very monotonous. The same routine day after day, everything on schedule, never a slip-up. Besides, it was so quiet, and since Cady's arm and leg had stopped hurting, she could have used a little more excitement and activity. But in spite of everything, the time passed fairly quickly. Cady was never bored, and people gave her all kinds of games that she could play by herself with her right hand. Nor did she neglect her schoolbooks, spending a certain amount of time on her homework every day. She had already been in the hospital for three months, but would soon be ready to leave. Her fractures hadn't been as serious as they had at first assumed, and the doctors thought it would be better for her, now that she had made some improvement, to convalesce further in a sanatorium.

So the following week Mrs. van Altenhoven packed Cady's things, and Cady and her mother were driven for hours in an ambulance that brought them to the sanatorium. There her days were even lonelier. She had visitors once or twice a week, but no Nurse Ank, and again everything was new and unfamiliar. Her one ray of hope was that she was definitely on the mend.

Once she'd settled into the sanatorium and the bandages had been removed from her arm, she started learning how to walk all over again. It was terrible! Supported by two nurses, she inched her way forward, barely able to put one foot in front of the other, and the ordeal had to be repeated every day. But the more she walked, the better it went, and her legs soon became used to moving again.

Then came the joyful day when she was feeling well enough and her walking had progressed to the point where she was allowed out in the park with a nurse on one side and a cane on the other.

Chapter 4

When the weather was nice, Cady and Nurse Truus, who always accompanied her, would sit down on a bench in the park and talk or read for a while, if they'd brought along a book. During the last few days, they'd also ventured out a few times into the adjoining woods, and since Cady enjoyed that much more, the nurse had no objections. Of course Cady did have to walk very slowly, and an unexpected movement often caused her pain, yet every day she longed once more for this half-hour out of doors, when she could imagine that she was well again.

After three weeks, when Cady knew every path in the woods like the back of her hand, the doctor asked her if she would be happy and pleased at the idea of being able to go out by herself. Cady was thrilled. "Can I really?"

"Yes, you can. Now, go on out there and don't let us ever see you here again," he joked.

So, when Cady was ready to go, she picked up her cane and went through the door alone. It was strange—she was so used to having Nurse Truus beside her. Still, on this first day she wasn't supposed to go any farther than the gate. After half an hour, the ward nurse saw her come in with her face lit up and her cheeks redder than usual.

"I see you enjoyed your walk! You must be glad to be rid of us!"

"You know I'm not," Cady replied. "But it's so nice to be able to do something on my own again!"

The nurse nodded sympathetically and advised her to go back to bed.

From then on, she could be seen out in the park every day, and soon things were going so well that she was also given permission to go beyond the gate.

The sanatorium was located in a very quiet neighborhood. There were hardly any houses, just a few villas about ten minutes away from the sanatorium and about ten minutes away from one another.

On one of the side paths, Cady had discovered a bench in the form of a log, and she brought along a few blankets to make it more comfortable. She now went there every morning to read or daydream. Often, when she had a book with her, it would slip out of her hands after only a few pages, and she would think to herself, "What do I care about that old book? Isn't it much nicer to sit here and look around? Isn't it better to think about the world and everything in it instead of reading about what's happening to some girl in a book?" Then she would take a look around, at the birds and the flowers, or let her eyes follow an ant scurrying over the ground with a tiny little stick, and she would feel happy. She dreamed of the time when she'd be able to run and jump and go wherever she wanted to, and came to the conclusion that her accident, which had brought her so much misery, also had its good side. Cady suddenly realized that here in the woods, in the sanatorium and in the silent hours in the hospital, she had discovered something new about herself. She had discovered that she was a person with feelings, thoughts and opinions of her own, completely independent of other people, who were individuals just like she was.

Why hadn't she realized that before? Why had it never occurred to her to think about the people around her, not even about her own parents?

What was it that Nurse Ank had said? "Perhaps your mother's been through so much that she prefers to avoid painful subjects." And hadn't she answered, "What does a daughter know about the lives of her parents?"

Where had her rather bitter answer come from, when she was sure she'd never thought about the matter before? And yet, wouldn't she say the same thing now? It was true, wasn't it? What does a child know about anyone's life? She could have said the same about her friends, her family, her teachers. What did she know of them other than the side they presented to the outside world? Had she ever had a serious talk with even one of them? Deep in her heart she was ashamed of herself for this, though she had no idea of how to go about getting to know any of these people better; and besides, she decided, what good does it do me to have their trust if I can't help them with their problems? And though she knew that she had not known how to help, she also knew that confiding in another person could be a great comfort and relief. Not long ago, she herself had missed having someone she could "really" talk to. Didn't this account for the oppressive loneliness she sometimes felt? Wouldn't it have weighed less heavily on her if she'd had a girlfriend to whom she could tell everything? Cady knew with utter certainty that she hadn't done enough for other people, but she was also sure that they had never given her so much as a second thought.

Cady looked up and realized that she hadn't been listening to a single sound the whole time she'd been sitting there. She quickly picked up her book, and in that one morning read more than she had ever read in the woods before.

Chapter 5

Cady had a naturally cheerful disposition and liked to talk. Still, the reason she was lonely was not because there were too few opportunities for her to confide in others.

No, that wasn't it. Her feeling of being alone had to come from somewhere else!

Oh, oh, she was lost in thought again. Cut it out, Cady, you've circled back to that same point so many times your head is starting to spin. Cady gave herself a mental nudge and had to laugh at how crazy it was: now that there was nobody to give her a good scolding and she apparently couldn't do without one, she had to scold herself.

Suddenly she looked up, having heard footsteps approaching. Never before had she encountered anyone on this little-used path. The footsteps came closer and closer, until a boy of about seventeen emerged from the woods. He nodded a friendly greeting and walked on.

"Who on earth could that be?" she wondered. "Maybe somebody from one of the villas? I suppose so, nobody else lives around here." After Cady had reached this conclusion, the subject was closed as far as she was concerned, and she forgot all about him until he passed by again the next morning, and every morning at exactly the same time for several weeks.

One morning, when Cady was seated on her bench as usual, the boy came out of the woods, stopped in front of her, held out his hand and said, "I'm Hans Donkert. Actually, I feel as if we know each other already, but perhaps it's time we introduced ourselves."

"My name is Cady van Altenhoven," Cady replied. "And," she added, "I'm glad you finally decided to stop."

"Well, you see, I didn't know if you'd think it was ridiculous for me to keep going by without saying a word, or for me to speak to you, and in the end I was just so curious that I took the plunge!"

"Do I look like the kind of person you should be afraid to talk to?" Cady inquired in a mischievous tone of voice.

"Now that I've seen you close up, no," Hans teased her back. "Anyway, I just wanted to ask you whether you've moved into one of the villas or whether you're a patient at the sanatorium . . . though that hardly seems likely," Hans added quickly.

"It doesn't?" Cady couldn't help asking. "Well, I am from the sanatorium. I broke my leg and badly injured my arm and foot, and I've been convalescing for six months."

"That bad, huh?"

"Yes, I was stupid enough to get hit by a car. But don't be alarmed—even you didn't think I looked like a patient!"

Hans did find it a bit alarming, but thought it advisable to avoid the subject. "I live in 'The Pines,' the house back that way," he said, pointing his forefinger in the direction from which he had come. "You might have thought it strange, seeing me go by here every day, but it's vacation time and I'm home from school, and every morning I go over to see one of my friends to keep from being bored."

Cady made a move to get up. Hans noticed and immediately offered her his hand, since she was having a little trouble rising from her seat. However, Cady stubbornly refused his assistance. "I'm sorry, but I've got to practice getting up on my own." Hans, who wanted to help in some way, took her book and used that as an excuse to escort the nice girl back to the sanatorium. They said goodbye at the gate as if they were old friends, so Cady was not at all surprised the next day when Hans arrived earlier than usual and sat down beside her on the log.

They talked about all kinds of things, though the conversation never went beyond the superficial, and Cady, who thought that Hans was incredibly nice, was sorry that they never touched on anything but everyday topics.

One morning they were sitting together on the log, not far from each other, and the conversation started to drag for the very first time. Finally, neither of them said another word, but they just sat staring into space. Cady, who had been engrossed in her own thoughts, suddenly looked up, since she had the feeling that she was being watched. Hans had been looking at the sweet face beside him for quite a while, but now their eyes met and they looked at each other longer than they had intended—until Cady realized what was happening and quickly looked down at the ground again.

"Cady," said the voice next to her. "Cady, can't you tell me what's going on inside you?"

Cady didn't answer, but thought for a moment. Then she said, "It's so hard, you wouldn't understand, you'd probably think it was childish." Her voice trailed off in sudden discouragement.

"Do you have so little trust in me? Do you think that I don't have thoughts and feelings that I usually keep to myself too?"

"I didn't mean to imply that I don't trust you, it's just so hard. I don't even know what I should tell you." They both looked down at the ground with the gravest of expressions. Cady noticed that Hans was extremely disappointed in her, and she felt so bad about it that she suddenly said, "Do you also feel like you're alone a lot of the time, even when your friends are close by? Alone deep inside you, I mean."

"I think everyone our age feels alone from time to time,

some more than others. I do too, but up to now I haven't been able to talk about it to anyone. Boys don't tell each other these kinds of things as easily as girls do. They're much more afraid of being misunderstood or of being laughed at."

He fell silent and Cady looked at him for a moment. Then she said, "I've thought about it so much. Why is there so little trust between people? Why are they so anxious to avoid 'real' words? Sometimes all it takes is a few sentences to clear up a problem or misunderstanding!"

Again neither of them spoke for a while. Then Cady suddenly seemed to have reached a decision. "Do you believe in God, Hans?"

"Yes, I certainly do!"

"I've been thinking about God quite a bit lately, though I've never told anyone before. When I was a little girl, my parents taught me to say a prayer every night before I went to bed. It became a habit, like brushing my teeth. I took God for granted. I mean, I never thought about Him, because all my wants and needs were taken care of. Now that I've had this accident and I'm often alone, I've had more than enough time to ponder all kinds of things. One of the first nights I was here, I got halfway through my prayers and realized that my mind was on very different matters. So I did something I'd never done before. I started thinking about the underlying meaning of the words and discovered that there's much more to this supposedly simple child's prayer than I ever suspected. Since that night, I've been saying other prayers, things that I myself thought were beautiful, not just a standard prayer. But a few weeks ago, I was halfway through my prayers again when a thought struck me like a bolt of lightning: 'Why should God help me now, in my hour of need, when I all but ignored Him in better days?' This question kept haunting me, because I knew that it would only be fair if God were to ignore my prayers in return."

"As far as that last bit is concerned, Cady, I can't say that I agree with you. When you were at home, leading your carefree life, you weren't reciting meaningless words on purpose, you just hadn't given God a lot of thought. Now that you're turning to Him because you're frightened and hurt, now that you're really trying to be the person you think you ought to be, surely God won't let you down. Have faith in Him, Cady. He has helped so many others!"

Cady gazed thoughtfully at the trees. "Hans, how do we know that God exists? Who or what is God? No one has ever seen Him. I sometimes have the feeling that all those prayers are being addressed to empty air!"

"If you're asking me who or what God is, I have only this to say: No one can tell you who God is or what He looks like, because no one knows. But if you're asking what God is, my answer would be: Take a look around you, at the flowers, the trees, the animals, the people, and then you'll know what God is. Those wondrous things that live and die and reproduce themselves, all that we refer to as nature—that's God. He made them all just the way they are, and that's the only image of Him you need. People have lumped this miracle together into one word: God. But any other name would do just as well. Don't you think so, Cady?"

"Yes, I understand all that, and I've also thought about it. Sometimes, when the doctor at the hospital said to me,

'You're getting better. I'm almost certain you'll make a full recovery,' I felt so grateful, and apart from the doctors and the nurses, who else should I feel grateful to but God? At other times, however, when I was in a lot of pain, I believed that what I was calling God was actually fate, and my mind kept going around in circles without ever arriving at an answer. But whenever I asked myself, 'Well, what exactly do you believe?,' I knew without a doubt that I believed in God. Quite often I ask God for advice, if that's the right term, and I know with utter certainty that the answer I'm given is the only right one. But, Hans, isn't it possible that the answer somehow comes from inside me?"

"As I already said, Cady, God has created mankind and every living thing just as they are. Our souls and our sense of what's good and right also come from Him. So the answer to your questions comes from within yourself, as well as from God, since He made you the way you are."

"You mean that God speaks to me through myself?"

"Yes, that's precisely what I mean. And now that we've discussed God, Cady, we've actually shared quite a few of our innermost thoughts. Give me your hand and let this be a sign that we'll always trust one another, and that if either of us should ever have any problems and want to talk about them, we'll know where to go!"

Cady promptly held out her hand, and so they sat, hand in hand, for a long time, while a delightful calm came over both of them.

Ever since their conversation about God, both Hans and Cady felt that they had struck up a friendship that went much deeper than any outsider would have guessed.

In the meantime, Cady was so used to writing down in her diary everything that went on around her that this gradually became the best way, aside from talking to Hans, to express her thoughts and feelings.

One day she wrote: "Even though I now have a 'real' friend, I'm not always happy and cheerful. Does everybody have such mood swings? Still, if I were always cheerful, I might not spend enough time thinking about all the things that are worth thinking about.

"Our conversation about God keeps running through my head. Often I'll be reading in bed or in the woods, and I'll think, 'What do you mean, God speaks through me?,' and I'll wind up having an entire discussion with myself.

"I believe that God speaks 'through me' because He gives each person a little bit of Himself before sending them into the world. It's this part of us that distinguishes between good and evil and answers our questions. This little bit of God is just as much a part of nature as the blossoming of flowers and the singing of birds.

"But God has also given people passions and desires, and these desires are in conflict with goodness and justice. As Hans said, 'Our sense of what's good and right also comes from God.'

"Does everyone really have this? What about criminals? I'm pretty sure they do too, except that little by little their desires have won out over goodness and justice and their passions have therefore become stronger than their sense of what's right. So can people destroy all the goodness God gave them? Can there be none of that goodness left? Or do even the worst criminals, the ones the world looks upon as wicked to the core, still have a bit of goodness deep down inside that might shine through someday?

"And yet not every sense of what's good and right can be trusted, for what else is war but two sides going to battle over what each thinks is right?

"War . . . how on earth did the subject of war come up? For weeks everybody has been saying that we're on the brink of war.

"But I'm not through yet.

"So far, all those who have tried to impose their version of what's right on others have failed. After a few years, or even longer, people always want their freedom and their own rights back. This is because having to obey one concept of right is inherently unjust. God has given each of us a unique sense of right, so when we are forced to live under someone else's for years and years, we run the risk of losing our own. But not everyone can be crushed. Sooner or later the longing for freedom is bound to assert itself.

"Without realizing it, I've gone from justice to freedom, but I believe that it is only when these two are combined that something great will happen.

"Who knows, perhaps one day people will listen more to that 'little bit of God'—known as a conscience—than to their own desires!"

Cady's Life: *Fragment*

The next morning was a typical, gray April day. It hadn't started to rain yet, but the barometer was as low as it could go. Cady didn't wake up until ten o'clock, and she listened as Nurse Ank described the circumstances of her fall in more detail. She was washed and given a little oatmeal, then she fell asleep again. And so it went for four whole days: Cady woke up from time to time, ate a bit and went back to sleep. She wasn't in a lot of pain, and except for having to lie still, she didn't feel uncomfortable.

On the afternoon of the fourth day, Cady was wide awake for the first time when her mother came to see her. Up till now Mrs. van Altenhoven had always found her daughter asleep, and had sat at her bedside for a quarter of an hour before going away again. Now she was surprised to be greeted cheerfully with: "So, Mom, did you finally decide to visit?"

"I've been coming here every day, you sleepyhead. You were never awake."

"I know. Nurse Ank said hello for you."

Mother and daughter had little to say to each other.

Cady asked about all her friends and neighbors, then the conversation began to flag. After half an hour, Mrs. van Altenhoven leaned over and gave Cady a kiss. "Bye-bye, I'll see you tomorrow!" And she sailed out the door. Cady's mother was not beautiful, though she did have an intelligent and determined face. Her long pointed nose and penetrating brown eyes gave her face a certain coldness, and when she fixed her gaze on someone, there was an unpleasant expression in them. But when she smiled, you could see a row of fine teeth, and then it no longer occurred to anyone to think of her face as cold. Cady had never given much thought to what her mother looked like, but she now noticed that her mother tended to waggle like a goose when she walked. Never in a thousand years would she have made the comparison to her mother's face, but she couldn't help chuckling and chiding herself for calling her mother a goose.

On the other hand, in the evenings, when it was visiting time, Cady was never sleepy. She waited impatiently in her bed for her father, who never neglected to bring her something—a bouquet of tulips or a bit of fruit—even if it was just something small. Cady adored these little gifts. The moment the door opened and Mr. van Altenhoven came in, Cady's eyes lit up, and he was always allowed to stay longer than her mother.

Cady's father was a calm, good-looking man with a thick head of gray hair and blue eyes, which made everyone who looked at him feel happy and warm. His gaze also worked like a magic potion on Cady. She and her father could sit quietly for hours, not saying a word, simply happy to be together.

Nurse Ank, the nurse who took care of Cady, always

wore a look of gratitude when she saw this kindly man, who came every day, without fail, to cheer up his daughter.

She didn't have the slightest bit of trouble with her little patient. Cady, who must have been in a great deal of pain, especially when she was being examined by the doctor, never complained. On the contrary, she was happy with everything.

Cady's Life: *Fragment*

It happened just as Nurse Ank said it would. On Sunday afternoon at three o'clock, Cady's first youthful visitor arrived. A tall girl, not at all pretty, but with a pleasant, cheerful face, asked at the desk for Caroline Dorothea van Altenhoven.

"Oh, you must mean that nice girl they call Cady. She's in Room 4, third door on the right."

Cady had won the heart of the desk clerk when she gave orders for a box of chocolates, which someone had given her, to be distributed throughout the hospital, so that the nurses and any of the patients allowed to eat them were given two bonbons each. As a result, even people Cady had never met referred to her as "that nice girl, Cady."

Meanwhile, the visitor walked down to Room 4 and knocked. Nurse Ank opened the door and said, "You must be Greet. Come in."

"Hello, Greet. Don't look so scared, I'm still in one piece!" Cady was overjoyed to see someone besides those grave-faced nurses for a change.

"Well, Cady, how do you feel?" Greet was noticeably embarrassed, so Nurse Ank, who was hoping she'd be a little more lively, left the room.

Later, on her way back, she heard peals of laughter from down the hall. She quickly opened the door and said, "Shh, keep it down a bit, girls."

"Oh, Nurse, I practically split my sides. You should hear what they've been up to at school. Such a shame I had to miss it." And she told the story, down to the last juicy detail, to Nurse Ank.

When Greet left at three-thirty, Cady was exhausted but happy to have had a visitor, and that was the main thing, since there was plenty of time to sleep.

In general, however, the weeks went by fairly monotonously.

Cady's Life: *Fragment*

On September 3 the peace and quiet in the sanatorium was disrupted for the first time since Cady's arrival.

At one in the afternoon, when she happened to be listening to the news on her earphones, she was horrified to hear the ANP begin its broadcast by reading Chamberlain's declaration of war on Germany. Cady had never been interested in politics, which is not surprising for a fourteen-year-old girl, and she wasn't the least bit moved by events taking place in faraway places. But she vaguely suspected that this declaration of war was somehow going to affect her too. When the rest hour was over, the nurse brought around the tea and told the other patients the news.

In Cady's ward, there were only patients who were well on the way to recovery. The day before the war broke out, a new woman had arrived and been assigned the bed next to Cady's. Except for "good morning" and "good night," Cady hadn't yet exchanged a word with this woman, but now they naturally got to talking. After the nurse's announcement, there had been exclamations of shock all over the room. Only the woman next to Cady had remained silent.

Cady couldn't help but notice. Nor could she ignore the tears that were soon streaming down the rather young-looking face and making it appear thoroughly sad and miserable. She didn't dare ask anything, for fear of disturbing her neighbor, who was wrapped up in her own thoughts. A little later in the day, Cady was reading when she heard sobs coming from the next bed. She quickly laid her book on her nightstand and gently inquired, "Shall I call the nurse? Are you not feeling well?"

The woman looked up. Her face was streaked with tears. She observed Cady for a moment, then said, "No, my dear. Don't bother. No nurse and no medicine can ease my pain."

This made Cady feel even sorrier for her. The poor woman looked so gloomy and dejected that she couldn't leave it at that. "Is there anything I can do to help?"

The woman, who had slumped back into her pillows, sat up again, dried her eyes with her handkerchief and this time gave Cady a friendly look. "I can see you're not asking out of mere curiosity. Even though you're very young, I'll tell you what's making me so sad." Her voice broke, she glanced around with unseeing eyes, then continued. "My son . . . I'm worried about my son. He's at a boarding school in England and was due home next month. But now . . ."

She was so overcome with sobs that she couldn't finish her sentence, so Cady filled in the rest: "Now he won't be able to come home?"

She received a faint nod in reply. "Who knows how long the war will last or what will happen over there. I don't believe all that talk about it being over in a couple of months. Wars always last longer than people think."

"But at the moment they're only fighting in Poland, aren't they? You mustn't be so afraid. After all, your son is being taken care of." Cady knew nothing about the boy, she had just wanted to respond in some way to the disheartened reply from the next bed.

But the woman apparently wasn't listening, for she said, "After every war, people always say, 'Never again, this was so terrible that we must avoid a recurrence at all costs.' But they always end up fighting again. People will never change. As long as they live and breathe, they'll always quarrel, and when there's peace, they'll go looking for something to quarrel about."

"I wouldn't know, I've never been through a war, but . . . we're not at war yet. So far we haven't gotten involved. Of course what you just told me about your son is unfortunate, though I'm sure you'll be reunited with him after the war. But wait a moment . . . Why can't your son come here? They haven't stopped all the boats between Holland and England, have they? Why don't you ask the doctor? He's sure to know. If your son leaves right away, he can still come home."

Never before had Cady seen a face change so dramatically from one minute to the next. "Do you really think so? That hadn't occurred to me. Oh, here comes the nurse, I'll ask her."

Cady and her neighbor beckoned the approaching nurse and she came over.

"Nurse," the woman asked, "do you know if they've stopped the boats between Holland and England?"

"They certainly haven't. Are you thinking about going to England?"

"Oh, no. That's not why I asked. Thank you very much, Nurse."

After casting another grateful glance at Cady, the woman turned away and began making plans to write to her son.

Cady's Life: *Continued*

Meanwhile, for the Jewish population life was going rapidly downhill. In 1942 the fate of many Jews hung in the balance. In July the Germans started sending call-up notices to sixteen-year-old girls and boys and taking them away. Luckily, they seemed to have overlooked Cady's friend Mary. Later, it wasn't just young people who had to go, but everyone. Throughout the fall and winter, Cady saw the most terrible things. Night after night the streets were filled with the sound of roaring trucks, screaming children and banging doors. Beneath the lamp, Mr. and Mrs. van Altenhoven and Cady looked at each other, and in their eyes was the question, "Who will be gone in the morning?"

One evening in December, Cady decided to visit Mary, in hopes of taking her friend's mind off things for a while. That evening, the streets were in a worse turmoil than ever. Cady had to ring the bell to the Hopkenses' three times and assure Mary, who peeked cautiously out the window, that it was safe to open the door. Mary led her in to where the whole family was sitting around in tracksuits with knapsacks on their backs, apparently just waiting. They were pale, and didn't say a word when Cady entered the room. Had they been sitting like this every night for months? Seeing all those pale and frightened faces was awful. With each bang of an outside door, a shock went through everyone in the room, as if the door to life itself were symbolically being slammed shut.

Cady left at ten o'clock. There was no point in staying, since she could neither help these people, who already seemed to be in another world, nor take their minds off their troubles. The only one who was functioning at all was Mary. She nodded at Cady from time to time and tried with all her might to get her parents and sisters to eat something.

Mary walked her to the door and bolted it behind her. Cady set off toward home with her flashlight in her hand. Before she'd gone even five steps, she stopped and listened. From around the corner she could hear the thud of boots, as if an entire regiment of soldiers were coming her way. It was impossible to make out anything in the darkness, but Cady knew all too well who belonged to the boots and what it meant. She flattened herself against a wall, switched off her flashlight and hoped the men wouldn't see her. Suddenly, however, a man holding a revolver came to a halt in front of her. He stared at her with steely eyes and a grim expression on his face. *"Mitgehen,"** was all he said, and immediately someone grabbed her and started to lead her away.

"I'm a Christian girl from a decent family!" she dared to say. She was trembling from head to foot and wondering

---

*"Come with me."

what this sinister man was planning to do with her. Despite the risk, she had to get him to look at her identity card.

"*Was ehrbar, zeig dein Beweis.*"*

Cady took it out of her pocket.

"*Warum hast du das nicht gleich gesagt,*"† said the man as he inspected it. "*So ein Lumpenpack,*"‡ he added.

And before she knew it, she was lying sprawled out on the street. The German, angry at his mistake, had given the "decent Christian girl" a vicious kick. Ignoring her pain and everything else, Cady picked herself up and hurried home.

After that night, a week went by before Cady had a chance to visit Mary again. But one afternoon she made the time, deciding not to worry about her homework or other engagements. Even before she arrived at the Hopkenses', she had a feeling she wouldn't find Mary at home, and sure enough, when she got there, the door was sealed.

A terrible feeling of despair came over Cady. "Who knows where Mary is now?" she thought. She turned on her heel and went home. Once there, she ran to her room, slammed the door, threw herself on the divan with her coat still on and thought about Mary, only Mary.

Why did Mary have to go while she was allowed to

---

*"What do you mean, decent? Show me your ID."

†"Why didn't you say so right away?"

‡"Such a shabby-looking girl."

stay? Why did Mary have to suffer this awful fate while she was free to enjoy herself? What was the difference between them? Was she any better than Mary? Weren't the two of them just the same? What crime had Mary ever committed? Oh, this had to be the most terrible injustice. Suddenly she saw Mary's frail figure before her, locked up in a cell, dressed in rags, with a sunken, emaciated face. Her eyes had become huge, and she was looking at Cady with such sorrow and reproach. Cady could stand it no longer. She fell to her knees and cried, cried so hard that her body shook with sobs. Mary's eyes kept staring at her, begging her for help, help that Cady knew she couldn't give.

"Forgive me, Mary. Come back . . ."

Cady no longer knew what to say or think. There were no words to describe the suffering she could so clearly see before her. Doors kept slamming over and over again in her ears, she could hear the crying children, she could see a squad of crude, armed men, like the one who had tossed her into the mud, and in their midst, helpless and alone, was Mary, Mary who was just the same as she was.

Ask Your Bookseller for These Bantam Classics

❧

A Connecticut Yankee in King Arthur's Court, Mark Twain, 0-553-21143-9

Life on the Mississippi, Mark Twain, 0-553-21349-0

The Prince and the Pauper, Mark Twain, 0-553-21256-7

Pudd'nhead Wilson, Mark Twain, 0-553-21158-7

20,000 Leagues Under the Sea, Jules Verne, 0-553-21252-4

Around the World in Eighty Days, Jules Verne, 0-553-21356-3

From the Earth to the Moon, Jules Verne, 0-553-21420-9

The Aeneid of Virgil, 0-553-21041-6

Candide, Voltaire, 0-553-21166-8

The Invisible Man, H. G. Wells, 0-553-21353-9

The Island of Dr. Moreau, H. G. Wells, 0-553-21432-2

The Time Machine, H. G. Wells, 0-553-21351-2

The War of the Worlds, H. G. Wells, 0-553-21338-5

The Age of Innocence, Edith Wharton, 0-553-21450-0

The Custom of the Country, Edith Wharton, 0-553-21393-8

Ethan Frome and Other Short Fiction, Edith Wharton, 0-553-21255-9

The House of Mirth, Edith Wharton, 0-553-21320-2

Summer, Edith Wharton, 0-553-21422-5

Leaves of Grass, Walt Whitman, 0-553-21116-1

The Accident, Elie Wiesel, 0-553-58170-8

Dawn, Elie Wiesel, 0-553-22536-7

Night, Elie Wiesel, 0-553-27253-5

The Picture of Dorian Gray and Other Writings, Oscar Wilde, 0-553-21254-0

The Swiss Family Robinson, Johann David Wyss, 0-553-21403-9

Early African-American Classics, 0-553-21379-2

Fifty Great Short Stories, 0-553-27745-6

Fifty Great American Short Stories, 0-553-27294-2

Short Shorts, 0-553-27440-6

GREAT AMERICAN SHORT STORIES, 0-440-33060-2

SHORT STORY MASTERPIECES, 0-440-37864-8

THE VOICE THAT IS GREAT WITHIN US, 0-553-26263-7

THE BLACK POETS, 0-553-27563-1

THREE CENTURIES OF AMERICAN POETRY, (TRADE) 0-553-37518-0,
    (HARDCOVER) 0-553-10250-8